Indian Cities

Raghavan Srinivasan is a chemical engineer (Madras University) and an MBA from McMaster University, Canada. He currently works as a development professional and has written a number of articles for print and online newspapers as well as international journals. He co-edits an online magazine called *Ghadar Jari Hai*. Raghavan is passionate about various aspects of Indian history and writes regularly on the same. His published books include *Rajaraja Chola* and *Yugantar*.

Quick and Concise

INDIAN CITIES

Ancient and Medieval

Best wishes!

S. Raghavan

Raghavan Srinivasan

hachette INDIA

First published in 2023 by Hachette India
(Registered name: Hachette Book Publishing India Pvt.Ltd)
An Hachette UK company
www.hachetteindia.com

ISBN 978-93-5731-250-9

Hachette Book Publishing India Pvt. Ltd
4th/5th Floors, Corporate Centre,
Plot No. 94, Sector 44, Gurugram 122003, India

Typest in Cambria 10/12 by Avishek Bhattacharya

Printed and bound in India
by Manipal Technologies Limited

MIX
Paper | Supporting responsible forestry
FSC™ C043100

To all those pioneering archaeologists
and historians who helped discover India's lost cities.

Contents

Preface

This reference book is written for those who are generally interested in India's history, her polity, art, architecture, literature, and other aspects but who don't have a full appreciation of her ancient and medieval cities.

To deep dive into all the Indian cities of importance spread over a period of five thousand years, with a huge geography and multiple cultures of subcontinental proportions, is impossible in the limited pages of this book. Therefore, some sort of selection is inevitable. The cities that have been chosen in this book are representative of all periods of Indian history from the Harappan Civilization to the late medieval period. Care has also been taken to represent as many dynasties, geographies, and cultures as possible so that the reader can savour this splendid heritage.

The urbanization process, the emergence of cities, started very early in the Indian subcontinent. The easiest way to present the story of these cities would have been to select twenty or thirty of the more important ones and deal with them as independent entities. Such a presentation has been attempted before. But besides lacking a presentation style, such a narrative would leave out important aspects of connections between these cities, such as geography, empires, culture, polity, and technology.

The narrative in this book groups major cities according to historical periods in which they thrived and also weaves into the narrative common elements of comparison, such as size, architectural features, technology, metallurgy, writing, food surpluses, transport, trade, relationship between cities, and their hinterlands, cultural complexity, social stratification, literature, agricultural surplus, political control, military organization, religious views, schools of thought, communication and exchange, and so on. Some of the cities which straddled many historical periods, such as Pataliputra and Madurai, have been covered in a particular period where they reached their peak and cross-referenced in others.

With this perspective in mind, we have presented twenty-five cities in this publication. Each section comes with an introductory note which enlightens the reader on the specific features of that period and about the basis for the selection of cities in that section.

What a city's features include in general:

- Architectural features (monuments, material, size, etc.)
- Technological (drainage, weights and measures, copper bronze, sailboats, ploughs, wheeled transport, specialization, etc.)
- Social (appropriation of agricultural surplus, concentration of wealth, funerary practices, food habits, etc.)
- Political (governance structure, political elite, class conflict, etc.)
- Centres of learning (writing, art, religion, etc.)
- Trade and commerce (internal and external)

Each section ends with a summary as well as a fact-check sheet, answers for which are provided at the end of the book.

A reference section is provided at the end. As one can see, the source material available is not as proliferate as we would have wished it to be. While recent archaeological surveys have made the picture of our ancient cities sharper, the archaeological evidence is still woefully inadequate for other periods. Available literature on these cities are, while following a stereotype, often tainted with the authors' own biases.

The coming into being of these ancient cities, the Indian urbanization experience, happened during an age of innovations. Their histories have been remarkable and fascinating, and therefore examining and presenting the facts systematically, in a concise form, has been an enjoyable experience for me.

CITIES OF THE HARAPPAN CIVILIZATION

(2600–1900 BCE)

FOR MORE THAN A CENTURY, ADVENTURERS AND ARCHAEOLOGISTS HAD WANDERED AROUND THE RUINS OF HARAPPA AND HAD SENSED SOME SIGNIFICANT HISTORICAL EVIDENCE BURIED UNDER THEM, BUT SOMEHOW, NEVER WENT FURTHER.

There have been groundbreaking discoveries in its cities of Mohenjo-daro and Harappa. Initially, the Harappan Civilization was dated according to the dates of the Mesopotamian Civilization. Therefore, several archaeologists tended to compare the two, keeping the Mesopotamian features as a benchmark. But since then, archaeological data has revealed that the Harappan Civilization was a distinct society that evolved on its own with its own characteristics.

1921

Discovery of Harappa

The profiles of various Harappan settlements and the understanding of networks connecting the cities, towns and villages are now clearer. Although

1922
Discovery of Mohenjo-daro

Harappan cities have some common features, they also have significant differences.

Since the first sites were discovered in the Indus Valley, they were given the name 'Indus Valley Civilization'. They are also called the 'Sindhu', 'Saraswati' Civilization since the sites existed along the rivers Sindhu and Saraswati basin located in the north-western part of South Asia. After the first sites were discovered, many others across Afghanistan, and in Punjab, Sindh, Baluchistan and North-West frontier of Pakistan have been unearthed. In India, the sites are spread over Haryana, Rajasthan, Jammu, Gujarat and Uttar Pradesh. The cities are now called the cities of the Harappan Civilization, based on the convention of naming an archaeological discovery on the first site identified. These cities have a lot in common, like overall architecture, housing, water and sanitation, red-black pottery, terracotta cakes, standard-sized bricks, and certain varieties of stone and copper artefacts.

The Harappan culture is usually discussed in three phases – the early phase, which was the formative phase; the mature phase or the urban phase; and the late phase, when the cities

> **THE ANCIENT CIVILIZATIONS**
>
> According to scholars, only four ancient civilizations have contributed to continuous cultural developments in the same region:
>
> - The Mesopotamia Civilization
> - The Egyptian Civilization
> - The Indus Valley Civilization
> - The Chinese Civilization

declined. Using radio-carbon dating techniques, the time frame for the urban phase has been determined as 2600–1900 BCE.

For some time, it was believed that Harappan-Mesopotamian trade was substantial. But recent discoveries have unearthed that long-distance trade from Harappan cities was not all that lively. Unlike Mesopotamia, the Harappan cultural zone was rich in raw materials and food sources. Diverse and well-developed crafts point to vibrant internal trade through organized merchant groups.

INDUS AND MESOPOTAMIAN CITIES: A COMPARISON

The Akkadian-Sumerian Civilization and Harappan Civilization are contemporary civilizations that had trade and cultural relations.

The Indus Valley Civilization is explicitly referred to by Sargon of Akkad (2250 BCE), who called the region 'Meluhha'. He confirms the presence of ships from Meluhha anchored at his capital city of Akkad.

This period corresponds to the mature Harappan phase (2600–1900 BCE). The main occupation of the city of Mohenjo-daro was from about 2350 BCE to 1900 BCE.

By all accounts, the Indus Civilization covered a much larger area than the Mesopotamian Civilization, stretching over an area of 1.2 million square km and dotted with thousands of settlements. In comparison, Mesopotamia occupied only about 65,000 square km. However, the largest cities in both the civilizations had comparable populations of about thirty to forty thousand inhabitants.

At the pinnacle of its existence, the Indus Valley Civilization comprised no less than fifteen hundred sites, housing a mammoth population of about five million. On the other hand, Mesopotamia had a population of only around 290,000 in the same period.

The Harappan Civilization and a roller-coaster ride to discovery

For almost a century, the Harappan Civilization played hide-and-seek with archaeologists.

> **ANCIENT EGYPT**
>
> One of the world's oldest and most powerful civilizations in the region for over 3,000 years, 'the ancient Egyptian' civilization left behind numerous monuments, documents and works of art that continue to fascinate scholars even today.

The first documented adventurer to chance upon the civilization was Charles Mason, an army deserter, who climbed the mounds of Harappa in 1826. He thought that it was the historical spot where Alexander the Great met King Porus in battle in the fourth century BCE.

Another traveller called Alexander Burnes entered the site in his travel log but could not figure out the real importance of the place.

Three decades later, in the 1850s, the site had an important visitor. He was Alexander Cunningham, an engineer in the East India Company and had a large appetite for archaeology. Though he

***Figure 1:** A panaromic shot of Harappa site*

conducted some excavations, the site did not make an impression on him. Two decades later when he revisited the site as director general of the Archaeological Survey of India (ASI), he dug out many artefacts such as stone tools, pottery, and a seal with a bull stamped on it. He could not decipher the lettering nor identify the bull as belonging to any known civilization.

The nineteenth century came to an end without the Harappan Civilization being discovered. The new ASI officers who visited the site did not have the drive to pursue serious archaeological excavations. Even eminent archaeologists like Pandit Hirananda Sastri and D.R. Bhandarkar underestimated the antiquity of the findings.

In the 1920s serious excavations started, but the significance of the site still remained a mystery. Finally in 1924, John Marshall, director general of ASI, announced a tremendous discovery that pushed India's civilized history about two thousand five hundred years back in time. It became apparent that India was one of the world's ancient civilizations along with the civilizations of Mesopotamia and Egypt.

The written and spoken word

We know nothing about the language that the Harappans spoke. The script they had used has, unfortunately, not yet been deciphered. There are about four hundred basic signs in it with variations. The direction of writing is from right to left. Generally, the inscriptions are found on seals (mostly made out of stone) and sealings (tablets of clay on which the seal was pressed down to make an impression). Inscriptions, though fewer, were also found on copper tablets, bronze implements, and small objects made of terracotta, stone, and faience. The seals may have been used in trade transactions and in official administrative work. The virtual disappearance of the script by 1700 BCE suggests both a close connection of writing with city life and the lack of sufficient downward percolation of writing.

Town planning: A lesson in city administration

The presence of baths in houses, public wells, bathing areas, and high-quality drainage speaks highly of the importance given to water and sanitation. A practice followed more than four thousand years back, it is something modern city administrations can learn from. It is observed that Harappan cities did not have scattered habitations outside the city walls, indicating a high level of town planning and provision of basic necessities for inhabitants.

> **EARLIEST DRAINAGE SYSTEM**
>
> The earliest sewers were constructed in Mohenjo-daro and in Rome, the first date back some 4,500 years and the other 2,700 years ago.

There has been a debate on what kind of state the Harappan Civilization was a part of. Did they follow the practice of a strong, centralized state? The absence of massive royal tombs, palaces and temples, and a clear-cut social differentiation that is often witnessed in Mesopotamian and Egyptian Civilizations casts doubt on the centralized model. Artefacts of various types, such as ornaments made of precious metals and semi-precious stones and seals, are found in all types of residences. The distribution of wealth, while not uniform, was not very uneven either.

All these facts do not, however, dismiss the existence of a state. The level of homogeneity among the cities and the well-developed trade network do suggest a level of administration and interaction

> **HARAPPAN CIVILIZATION DID NOT HAVE A STRONG, CENTRALIZED STATE. HOWEVER, THERE IS EVIDENCE THAT SUGGESTS THE PRESENCE OF A STATE IN ITS FORMATIVE STAGE.**

between the cities. One answer could be the existence of a state in the formative stage; it ensured a level of cultural homogeneity and a common script.The relations between states and rural areas and general governance in Harrapan Civilization is still being researched; a lot of it is still subject to speculation.

The downward spiral

In the late Harappan phase (1900–1300 BCE), the cities declined and there was an eastward and southward migration of the population. The civilization became diffused, and many rural sites emerged. Though many reasons have been offered for the decline of the civilization, none have been proved beyond doubt. The decline could have been brought about by various factors such as floods and drought, rivers shifting their course, or tectonic movements resulting in major climatic changes. Reduction in trade and breakup of trade networks are also cited as possible determinants. However, the decline of the Harappan Civilization due to an Aryan invasion has been ruled out since there is no archaeological evidence of major battles and destruction of life.

Now let's look at four important Harappan cities and illustrate their common and divergent features both.

Figure 2: *Bricklaying skills of the city's masons*

Mohenjo-daro

Approximately a year after Harappa was discovered, in the year 1922, R.D. Banerji, an officer of the Archaeological Survey of India, discovered ruins of a city. On further investigation, it was revealed that the place had remained unknown for around 3,700 years and was one of the largest cities of the Indus Valley Civilization. It was subsequently named Mohenjo-daro, or 'Mound of the Dead'.

> **CITADEL**
>
> A citadel is the fortified area of a town or a city. The word is derived from Italian cittadella, which means 'small city'.
>
> The Indus Civilization featured some of the earliest examples of citadels and cities like Mohenjo-daro and Harappa featured prominent citadels.

Mohenjo-daro lies in Sindh Province of Pakistan, near the Indus River. The city consists of two mounds. The western mound is smaller but higher and the eastern mound is lower but larger. Estimations suggest that the size of the city would have been about 2 square km. And the population of the lower city may have been around forty one thousand two hundred and fifty.

The western mound, called the citadel, is built on an elevated mud-brick platform almost 12 metres above the ground level. And stretched 400 x 200 square metres in size. We have no definite idea whether the elevated platform was for defence purposes or just a part of the design.

The buildings on the citadel consist of the Great Bath, granary, and college of priests. Both the elevated citadel and the lower town, have a fortification wall around them and a tower.

The city is divided into major blocks by four streets and numerous smaller streets and alleys.

Mohenjo-daro: An engineering marvel

The streets, houses, and buildings display a measure of the considerable engineering skills of the Harappans. The Great Bath, for instance, consists of a wide staircase leading down to a tank. The floor and walls of the tank are made of perfectly fitted bricks, lined with gypsum mortar. A thick layer of bitumen along the sides makes the tank water-tight, which can be considered as one of the earliest specimens of waterproofing in the world.

ELABORATE ARRANGEMENTS FOR DRINKING WATER AND BATHING. RITUALS OR PERSONAL HYGIENE?

The fact that some houses reached a height of 5 metres or more is a testament to the strength of the bricks and the bricklaying skills of the city's masons. This is evident in other Harappan cities too. Several styles of bricklaying were adopted, which allowed for the walls to bear the extraordinary load. It's interesting to note that the bricks were of a standard size, showing that construction technology had reached an admirably professional level.

***Figure 3:** Archaeological remains at Mohenjo-daro*

> **THE GREAT BATH**
>
> The great bath consists of a wide staircase leading down to a tank. A thick layer of bitumen along the sides makes the tank watertight, which is one of the earliest specimens of waterproofing in the world

Houses were of different sizes, but their layout was similar. All of them had rooms surrounding a central courtyard. Doorways and windows usually opened towards the side lanes. Some had staircases that led to a second floor as well as thick walls. The roofs were supported by wooden beams while doors and windows were made of wood and mats. Doors were painted with simple designs. Windows had shutters and some even had latticework. Carved alabaster and marble latticework have been discovered among the ruins in the city.

Some of the large houses had small houses attached to them, indicating that they may have been used as servants' quarters in wealthy households.

State-of-the-art sewage system that modern Indian cities could learn from

When one notices that many houses in the city had their own bathing areas and toilets, one marvels at the excellent drinking water and sanitation arrangements of Mohenjo-daro. The floor of the bathing area was constructed of tightly fitted bricks sloping gradually to drain out the water. Drainpipes took the water out to a larger sewage drain.

Toilets ranged from a simple hole in the ground above a cesspit to more elaborate designs. Big pots sunk into, the floor with a small hole in the base served as commodes. And of course, the toilets and drains would have had to be cleaned regularly.

Separate chutes ensured that sewage and drainage water did not get mixed up. In buildings that had a second storey, drainage pipes ran inside the walls and opened just above the main drain in the streets.

The street drains were made of baked bricks and merged into larger drains in the main streets. Corbelled arches made of brick or stone slabs covered the main drains indicating a higher level of drainage design and capacity to perform regular maintenance so that the drains did not choke.

The city had elaborate arrangements for drinking water and bathing, emphasizing the importance given to personal hygiene. Whether religious rituals made bathing mandatory or a concern for personal hygiene made the Harappans build frequent bathing facilities is a question that needs investigation. Most of the water requirements of Mohenjo-daro came from its large number of wells.

In addition to a well-planned drainage system, Mohenjo-daro had a properly laid-out street and side-lane system.

Talented craftsmen and bustling workshops

Many occupational groups lived in the city, such as craftsmen, fisher-folk, merchants, architects, carpenters, masons, sculptors, boat makers, well diggers and shopkeepers. The neat layout of the city suggests the presence of efficient sweepers and refuse collectors. And to manage a city of this size, there must have been administrative officers too.

THE PRESENCE OF THE GREAT GRANARIES AND THE CITADELS POINT TO THE EXISTENCE OF PRIEST-KINGS – SIMILAR TO HOW IT WAS IN EGYPT.

Terracotta net sinkers and arrow points found at Mohenjo-daro and Harappa suggest that hunters and fisher-folk would have lived in the city quarters.

The houses vary in size suggesting differences in wealth and status. At one place, there are remains of a large building. Many seals and fragments of a stone sculpture depicting a seated man with a shawl over his shoulder, similar to the statues of a 'Priest-king' that have been unearthed in other areas. While nothing is conclusive, this building could have been a temple or the residence of a powerful leader. And in another area, remains have been found of a double row of houses consisting of a single room with a bathroom in front and one or two smaller rooms in the back.

In the lower town, many workshops manufacturing copper, beads, dyes, and pottery have been identified.

HARAPPAN POTTERY: A STANDARDIZED ART MARVEL

The Harappan civilization can be credited for a large range of standardized, mass-produced pottery. In the mature Harappan phase, pottery-making reached a higher technical finesse than earlier. The pots were fired in both closed and open-fired kilns. Most pottery was turned on wheels and displayed a bright red slip with motifs in black. The pottery was of different shapes and sizes ranging from tumblers used to drink water or beverages to large storage and cooking vessels. Some of the pottery show the earliest products of the technique of glazing in the world. Relatively plain pottery may have been used for day-to-day needs such as cooking and storing water and in poorer homes. Other elaborately painted pots may have been used in religious rituals and in prosperous homes. Most cooking pots have a strong base and a sturdy rim.

Figure 4: The priest-king

A bronze statuette believed to that of a 'Dancing Girl', 10.5 centimetres high and about four thousand five hundred years old, was discovered in Mohenjo-daro in 1926. It is now housed in the National Museum, New Delhi.

Archaeologists like Mortimer Wheeler and John Marshall have provided different interpretations of the statuette. But its discovery confirmed that the city had specialists in metal blending, casting, and other sophisticated methods of working with metal ore. It also shed light on the fact that entertainment, especially dance, was a part of their culture.

Female figurines of the Mother Goddess

There is a tendency to connect Harappan religion to later Hinduism but as of now, there has been no confirmation. If the Harappan script gets deciphered, we may have a conclusive answer to this puzzle.

There has been, however, a confirmation of worship of female goddesses. The Harappan Civilization was predominantly agricultural, and many terracotta female figurines called 'mother goddesses' have been unearthed. One should keep in mind, though, that not all female figurines can be associated with goddesses, but some do have religious or cultic significance.

Female figurines that have a religious significance are slim with an unmistakable fan-shaped head dress and a short skirt.

These figurines are heavily ornamented with necklaces, bangles, earrings, and others. The fact that they were not situated in temples and that mostly broken remnants have been recovered suggest that they were votive offerings rather than goddesses.

> **DANCING GIRL**
>
> Excavated in 1926 in Mohenjo-daro,the bronze sculpture depicts a nude young woman, with a coiled hairstyle and bangles adorning her arms. The statue was named 'Dancing Girl' based on the assumption of her profession and shows the expertise of the people making bronze works during the Harappan Civilization.

A male god has also been identified in a steatite seal, popularly called the Pashupati seal. It is so named because the figure is surrounded by many wild animals, such as the elephant, rhinoceros, water buffalo, and tiger. Whether the male figure is three-headed and ithyphallic (with erect penis) and whether he is related to Shiva of later Hindu mythology are the questions we don't yet have the answers to.

Minor conflicts, but majorly a politically stable place

We can assume that conflict would have been a part of life in the cities. When people live together, there are bound to be disagreements! But interestingly, many archaeologists have observed that weapons have not been the dominant component of artefacts found. Some terracotta reliefs do depict conflicts. But the elements of warfare do not seem to be the dominant factor in this culture. However, walls surrounding the lower and upper cities do indicate a certain requirement to defend from external aggression.

Historians such as Piggott suggested that the Harappan state was highly centralized and controlled by autocratic Priest-kings ruling from the twin capitals of Mohenjo-daro and Harappa. The idea behind this assumption is the fact that Mohenjo-daro and Harappan cities had a common script, standard weights and measures, pottery, urban planning, public works, and granaries.

At the end, one can safely assume that there may have been centralized control and classes at some level of development of the cities. There is little evidence of a supreme God or a common religion. The Harappan polity could very well have been a chiefdom, somewhere between a tribal society and a modern state.

It is also possible that the rulers might have been a coalition of different clans. The square stamp seals found at Mohenjo-daro and other cities can be interpreted as totemic symbols for different ruling clans. The seals of the unicorn, humped bull, elephant, water buffalo, rhinoceros, humpless bull with short horns, goat, antelope, crocodile, and hare are the different symbols. At Mohenjo-daro, over sixty per cent of the seals have the unicorn motif.

Harappa

While mounds of Mohenjo-daro covered 3 sq. kms, the mounds of Harappa cover just about half the area. The remains are situated hardly 10 kms away from the Ravi river. The elevated citadel mound lies on the western side of the ruins. In the south-east there is a larger lower area which served as the lower town. Somewhere near the citadel lies the burial ground used in the mature Harappan phase. The citadel is an impressive parallelogram-shaped structure containing several towers and gateways, enclosed by a mud-brick wall. Unlike the Mohenjo-daro citadel structures whose profiles

NO SIGNIFICANT WEAPONS HAVE BEEN FOUND FROM HARAPPAN SITES. HOW DID THEY FIGHT WARS?

could be made out by archaeologists, those in Harappa are considerably damaged.

Chronology of Harappa

1900–1300 BCE	Late Harappa Phase
1900–1800 BCE	Transitional to Late Harappa
2600–1900 BCE	Mature Harappa Phase
2200–1900 BCE	Harappa Phase C
2450–2200 BCE	Harappa Phase B
2600–2450 BCE	Harappa Phase A
2800–2600 BCE	KotDiji Phase
3800–2800 BCE	Pre-Harappan Ravi aspect of the Hakra phase

Original excavations at the site were initiated by the British colonial archaeologist Sir John Hubert Marshall in 1921.

Several remains of structures have been discovered north of the citadel complex. In all likelihood this area housed the quarters of craftsmen. One walled quarters unearthed had no less than fifteen units, each unit built with a room at the back and a courtyard in the front.

Further north, eighteen circular brick platforms were discovered. These are likely to be platforms erected for threshing barley and other grains. Further north, archaeologists found granary-like structures but no evidence has been found to confirm the nature of these structures.

There is a large open area in the lower town which could have functioned as a customs area for goods coming into the city. The lower town also had many manufacturing units. Just outside the southern gateway there were living quarters equipped with baths and drains, which may have been used by travellers as guest houses.

Growing from a small settlement to a capital city

The ancient city of Harappa has a history of almost five thousand years starting from 3800 BCE and stretching up to 1500 BCE. The modern city of Harappa still exists, standing above some of the ancient ruins.

At its peak the city covered about one square km, but it could have been bigger considering that much of the ancient site could have been washed away by the Ravi River. The monuments that are left now, as underscored earlier, are the citadel, the granary and a few cemeteries.

As can be seen from the box on chronology, the city of Harappa developed over many phases. The earliest is called the Ravi aspect, when Harappa began as a small settlement with a few workshops where craftsmen made agate beads.

In the next Kot Diji phase, the Harappans could manufacture sun-baked bricks to build city walls and houses and layout streets on a grid pattern where wheeled carts driven by bulls transported heavy commodities in and out of the city. Richer and poorer cemeteries displayed the first traces of economic disparity and social ranking. The first evidence of writing and the use of square stamp seals used in trade appeared in this phase.

During the mature Harappan phase, the city might have risen to the status of a capital city of the region. Unlike in Mesopotamia, Harappa did not have hereditary kings. The city was rather ruled by an elite consisting of landowners, merchants and religious heads. During this period, baked brick is used in large quantities especially in structures which required water proofing. Drains and wells were constructed. Faience and steatite bead product ion flourished. Tablets with scripts written on them were widely used for trade and administrative purposes.

Best of both worlds–an agricultural and manufacturing hub

The city of Harappa would have very likely been both a manufacturing and agricultural centre. Many grains such as wheat and barley and other food items such as millets, sesamum, watermelon seeds, peas and dates have been found in the site. Remains of marine catfish and horse bones have been discovered.

The craftsmen in the city manufactured a wide range of goods including ceramics and pottery. A number of pottery kilns have been located indicating their mass production. The city also housed a number of copper furnaces. The inhabitants valued metal objects which they buried in hoards. Various types of copper tools have also been unearthed. The city craftsmen also produced exquisitely designed gold and silver jewellery. Bead making was also an important occupation. Recent excavations have also indicated the presence of spinning wheels and the weaving of baskets of reed and thatch.

Dholavira

Dholavira, the fifth largest of the eight major Harappan sites, and the southern centre of the Harappan Civilization, is located at the Rann of Kutch, in Gujarat. About 120 acres in area, Dholavira was discovered in 1967–68 by J.P. Joshi of the ASI. The water levels may have been higher in those times, allowing boats to row up to the city from the coast.

DHOLAVIRA IS AN OUTSTANDING EXAMPLE OF URBAN PLANNING, MULTI-LAYERED FORTIFICATIONS AND SOPHISTICATED WATER RESERVOIRS. THESE CHARACTERISTICS GIVE THE PLACE A UNIQUE POSITION.

According to recent research, the city had been occupied from around 3500 BCE (pre-Harappan) till about 1800 BCE (early part of late Harappan), thus making it older than the port-city of Lothal.

> **STONE WALLS**
>
> Dholavira buildings were built of stone; in Mohanjo-daro, they were made of brick.

Buildings and monuments reveal a large-scale use of sandstone and mud-brick, a feature unique to the Harappan cities of Gujarat. The city has three divisions – the citadel, the middle town and the lower town.

The citadel and the middle town boasted defence arrangements, gateways, buildings, streets, wells, and large open spaces.

A castle towers over the citadel and is protected by double ramparts. The bailey, or the official quarters, is situated next to the castle. The remains of the settlements have been found even beyond the walls, suggesting that the city and its suburbs could have been bigger than what the archaeological findings suggest.

A large open area called the 'stadium', lying between the castle–bailey area and the middle town, may have been used for special ceremonial occasions.

Lying near the coast, the city must have been an important midway point on the busy maritime trade routes.

While Harappan cities have many common features, the most striking difference of Dholavira buildings is that they are built of stone, in contrast to Mohenjo-daro, where buildings are made of brick.

Dholavira is flanked by two stormwater channels: the Mansar in the north and the Manhar in the south.

Conserving water in a desert

Unlike Mohenjo-daro, Dholavira was situated in a desert area. In order to maintain the standards of Harappan cities when it comes to water and sanitation, the residents of Dholavira had to resort to rainwater harvesting and other water conservation methods.

In the words of Bisht, who retired as joint director-general of the ASI, 'The kind of efficient system of Harappans of Dholavira developed for conservation, harvesting and storage of water speaks eloquently about their advanced hydraulic engineering, given the state of technology in the third millennium BCE.' The sophisticated water conservation system of channels and reservoirs built of stone is the earliest found anywhere in the world.

Archaeologists have unearthed massive reservoirs for storing fresh water brought by rains or from nearby rivulets. Streams were dammed to collect water for the dry season. Sixteen or more reservoirs have been discovered, a few among them quite large. The reservoirs are about 7 metres deep and 79 metres long.

Like other Harappan cities, the city had planned bathing infrastructure. Bathing tanks were constructed with steps descending inwards. In 2014, a rectangular stepwell measuring 73 metres long x 29 metres wide x 10 metres deep was discovered. This is three times bigger than the Great Bath of Mohenjo-daro.

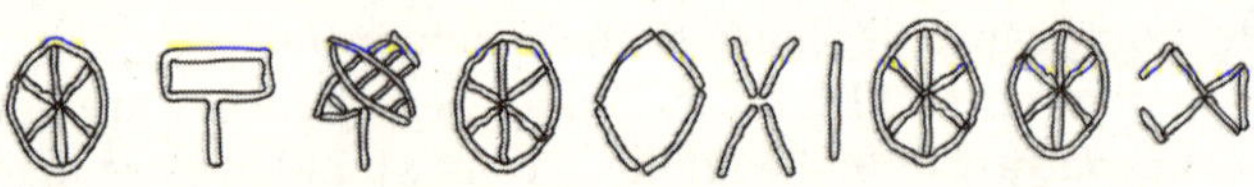

Figure 5: *Ten Indus characters from the northern gate of Dholavira*

THE DHOLAVIRA SIGNBOARD: A SIGNIFICANT DISCOVERY

Among the significant discoveries at Dholavira is the Dholavira Signboard. It has ten large symbols on a wooden board. The wood had decayed but the arrangement of letters was visible because of the gypsum used. The inscription is one of the longest Indus script inscriptions discovered anywhere. This signboard has been used by scholars to argue that the Indus script was indeed a complete language script and the Harappans, or at least a part of them, were literate. A four-letter inscription in large size engraved on sandstone has also been found in this city. It is the first of such inscription on sandstone at any of the Harappan sites.

Kalibangan

Kalibangan, a town located on the banks of the Ghaggar River in Hanumangarh District, Rajasthan, was a major provincial capital of the Indus Valley Civilization. The site was discovered by Luigi Pio Tessitori, an Italian Indologist (1887–1919) and in Kalibangan, the Indus Valley culture extended from the proto-Harappan age (3500 BCE–2500 BCE) to the Harappan age (2500 BCE–1750 BCE). And by around 2900 BCE, the region developed into a planned city.

The city is distinguished by its unique fire altars and the 'world's earliest attested ploughed field'. It evolved into a planned city at around 2900 BCE.

Amlānand Ghosh, Ex. Director General, ASI, was the first person to recognize this site as Harappan and mark it out for excavations. Mohenjo-daro and Kalibangan have a similar layout, made up of a raised citadel complex and a lower city.

Excavations in the site unearthed two mounds spread over half a kilometre. On the western side is the smaller mound, nine metres high and known as the citadel. Interestingly, the eastern mound, which is higher (12 metres) and bigger than the western mound is called the lower city. A smaller, third mound was also discovered. It has many fire altars. Both the citadel complex and lower town were fortified.

> **BLACK BANGLES**
>
> One of the major sites of the Indus Valley Civilization, *Kalibangan* literally means 'black bangles'. It derives its name from the countless weather-stained fragments of black bangles that were found at the mounds' surface.

The excavations revealed two cultural layers. The upper one (Kalibangan I) belongs to the Harappan culture, having the characteristic grid layout of a metropolis. The lower one (Kalibangan II) belongs to the early Harappan stage.

Figure 6: *Kalibangan II Main street*

The considerable heap of bangles of terracotta, shell, alabaster, steatite, and faience at the site, which gives the city its name, indicate that bangle making was an important occupation. Other interesting artefacts such as an ivory comb, a copper buffalo or bull, a stone phallic emblem with a base, and a terracotta fragment incised with a horned figure indicate a certain level of skill in crafting such objects.

The chessboard blueprint of Kalibangan

Some residential buildings, perhaps of the elite or of the priests who performed the fire rituals, are situated in the northern half of the citadel. These houses stand a bit away from the fortified walls, perhaps to provide some privacy to the residents. The space between the fortification wall and the houses were paved with bricks.

It appears that from the very beginning, the houses in the city were built of mud bricks of standard size. The employment of baked brick of the same size and shape were confined to drains, wells, sills, and bathing platforms. In the typical chessboard plan that characterizes most Harappan cities, each house faced two, if not three, streets and consisted of a courtyard with as many as six to seven rooms aligned on two or three sides. The entrance to the house was either through a courtyard or a corridor running between a row of rooms, and located usually on the lane side, and not the main street. Some houses had single panel doors and a stairway indicating an upper floor. There was a well in some courtyards, indicating joint use by more than one family. Some houses had a fire altar too.

> **HOW WAS THE FOOD COOKED?**
>
> During excavations, presence of ovens, both of the underground and above ground variety, was found. It closely resembled the present-day tandoors of the region.

There were no remains of residences outside the city walls indicating that either all residents had a house inside the city or the city was never allowed to grow beyond its walls.

The citadel had a thoroughfare running north to south. The lower city had four arterial thoroughfares running north to south and three running east to west. While the former ran without a break, the latter appeared to be delivery or entrance lanes for a colony of houses. Remains of other smaller cities have been found that served only certain blocks of houses. It is noteworthy that the width of the thoroughfares and streets were always a multiple of 1.8 metres and ranged from 1.8 to 7.2 metres. And to avoid damage from the vehicular traffic, fender posts were provided at some street corners, much like modern cities!

While corbelled drains made of bricks have been found on the citadel mound, the lower town does not have street drains of the type found in Mohenjo-daro. The sewage from houses was discharged into troughs or large jars buried in the ground outside.

DURING EXCAVATION, EXISTENCE OF CYLINDRICAL PITS LINED WITH LIME PLASTER WERE ALSO FOUND. THEY MIGHT HAVE BEEN USED TO STORE DRINKING WATER.

While barley appeared to be the stable staple, remains of wheat were also discovered. No remnants of rice were found.

A significant finding which distinguishes Kalibangan from Mohenjo-daro is the presence of fire altars. These altars suggest fire worship and throw some light on the religious practices of the Harappan civilization.

Kalibangan is also the only Indus Valley civilization site where there is no evidence to suggest the worship of the Mother Goddess.

In the citadel complex, several raised platforms of mud bricks, separated from each other by corridors, have been discovered. These platforms could be accessed by stairs. Remnants of oval shaped fire pits constructed of burnt bricks are present on these platforms, with sacrificial posts and terracotta cakes. Such altars are not present only in the citadel, but also in some houses in the lower town. The public altars could have been used for religious purposes by the entire community. Remnants of animals in these fire altars suggest animal sacrifice. Public altars have also been found in another separate area of the city. Very near the fire altars, remnants of a well and bathing place have been found, indicating that a ceremonial bath might have been an integral part of the rituals.

SOME HOUSES IN KALIBANGAN HAVE BEEN FOUND TO CONTAIN FIRE ALTARS. WHAT DO YOU THINK IT SIGNIFIES?

The burial grounds of Kalibangan

Harappan cemeteries were located at Kalibangan. The most common burials are those where the corpse is laid down straight with head northwards in a simple rectangular or oval pit. Grave goods included pottery, ornaments, food, and other items, in moderate quantities, indicating that they didn't see much point in wasting material on the dead.

The presence of symbolic burials with grave goods but no corpses were also discovered in Kalibangan. Pots and utensils were placed around the main pot, the urn. There were also symbolic burials in rectangular or oval pits containing only pottery and other funerary objects. These cemeteries had no skeletal remains.

Lothal

> **WHAT'S IN A NAME?**
>
> It is believed that Lothal is made up from the combination of two words; Loth and Thal, which in Gujarati means, 'the mound of the dead.'

Today the remnants of Lothal lie nearly 20 km away from the sea. But at the time of the Harappan civilization, it served as a port where vessels from the Gulf of Cambay sailed up to its wharves.

The settlement, however, is modest, comprising roughly 0.15 square km. The city is rectangular with a surrounding wall made of mud and burnt bricks. A burial ground lies outside the city walls. On the southern side of the settlement, a citadel exists, on an elevated mud-brick platform.

The ASI discovered Lothal in 1954 and the remains point to an existence of residential buildings, streets, bathing areas, and drains

***Figure 7:** Ruins of Lower Town at Lothal*

Figure 8: Lothal dockyard

similar to the ones seen in other Harappan cities. Just outside the residential area lies a warehouse; it might have been used for storing and packing goods before being loaded on to seafaring vessels. Among the remains are sixty-five terracotta sealings carrying different impressions of Harappan seals, showing that the port was a part of the civilization.

For a small city, it had a few large residential houses containing four to six rooms and equipped with bathrooms, a large courtyard, and accompanied by a verandah. Some of the houses had fire altars too.

After studying the remains of finished and unfinished artefacts, it was deduced that the city housed artisans such as coppersmiths and bead makers. The city also had a bazaar area lined with shops.

A differentiating feature of Lothal, from the Harappan cities we have seen so far, is its famed dockyard. The inhabitants had constructed a trapezoidal basin of roughly 7,800 square metres. All around the basin were walls constructed of mud bricks. The dockyard had a sluice gate to control the water level. On the western flank of the basin there is a platform constructed using

LOTHAL IS THE ONLY HARAPPAN CITY WITH DOCKYARDS.

mud brick, which perhaps served as a wharf where ships unloaded their goods. Though not conclusively proved, the dockyard is sometimes believed to be the world's oldest.

A famed trade state bustling with activity

From all accounts, Lothal was a trade centre bustling with activity, with its shipments in beads, gems, and valuable ornaments. The goods reached far corners of the globe such as West Asia and Africa. It is to the credit of the artisans that the tools they used for bead-making and metallurgy have stood the test of time and are in vogue even today. Among the workshop remains found at Lothal, some belonged to copper workshops. Metal objects were also found here containing a high level of iron, which suggests that the craftsmen in the city had some familiarity with iron smelting.

The existence of river transport in Harappan cities located along the seacoast or on riverbanks has been confirmed by symbols of boats carved or moulded on tablets and seals. Clay models of boats have been discovered at Lothal. The boats were quite sophisticated and had cabins and ladders to help climb to the top and a seated platform at the high point of the stern.

One issue that has intrigued archaeologists is whether horses existed in Harappan cities in those times. Even if horse remains were found, its cultural layer and species have to be confirmed. The bones of horses and the Asiatic wild ass (also called the half ass, or *Khur* in the local language) are difficult to distinguish. Horse remains have been detected in Lothal, besides other cities such as Harappa. However, horses may not have been domesticated in large numbers in that period.

Standardization in crafts reflects high level of social organization

Similar to other Harappan cities, we find, in Lothal as well, a high level of standardization in crafts. An ivory scale was among the important discoveries in Lothal. The high level of standardization could have played an important role in maintaining a relatively uniform social order in the civilization. The city used standard units for both weights and measures.

Standard weights made of different materials have been found in many sites. The system that Harappans used was binary for the smaller weights category. In the higher weights category, the decimal system was used.

The use of standard weights has been interpreted by scholars in different ways. One possibility is that the entire region was centrally controlled by merchant groups or the ruling houses. On the other hand, it could have been the result of hereditary groups of craftsmen migrating to other areas in the Harappan belt, bringing about a certain level of standardization. It is also possible that trade guilds or corporate groups had established a network among themselves across the Harappan cities. Whatever the reason may be, the standardization reflects a high level of social organization and trade.

Among the excavated objects, a complete set of terracotta gamesmen was found. And the realistic portrayal of human beings and animals in crafting toys and other objects reveals a certain level of sophistication. The images of men and women suggest a good understanding of anatomy. Toy carts with wheels and drawn by animals have also been found.

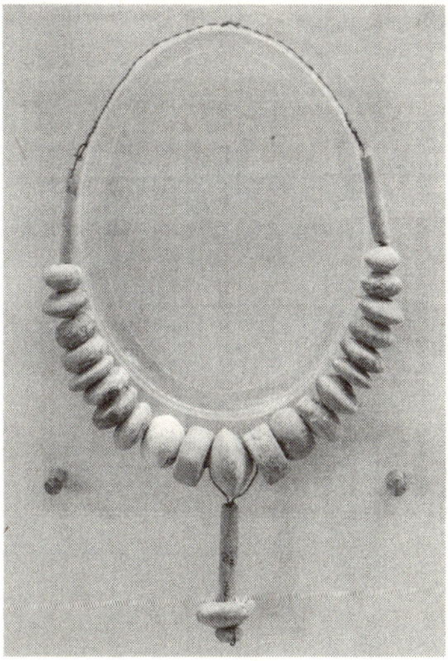

Figure 9: *Terracotta Bead garland found by ASI at Lothal*

Cities of the Harappan civilization

Feature	Mohenjo-daro	Harappa	Dholavira	Kalibangan	Lothal
Size (sq kms)	3	1.5	1	0.25	0.15
Population	40,000	23,500			15,000
Layout	Raised citadel complex and a lower town	Same	Three parts – citadel, middle town and lower town	Same	Citadel complex is located within the main settlement
Water supply	Wells	Wells and tank	Water reservoirs lined with stone		
Drainage	Terracotta drain-pipes	Terracotta drain-pipes			
Distinctive features, monuments, artefacts	The Priest-King		Water harvesting and management system	Clusters of black bangles	The dockyard
Female figurines	Large numbers	Large numbers			
Building material	Fired bricks	Fired bricks	Extensive use of sandstone	Fired bricks	Fired bricks

Takeaways

- The cities in the Harappan Civilization were spread over three phases: early Harappan, mature Harappan and late Harappan.
- The cities thrived most in the mature Harappan phase.
- Harappan cities represented the first urban culture in South Asia.
- The cities manufactured a number of products, practised a variety of crafts and were part of extensive trade networks.
- Unlike contemporary Mesopotamia, the Harappan cultural zone was rich in raw materials and food sources, and therefore, self-sufficient. Diverse and well-developed crafts point to vibrant internal trade through organized merchant groups.
- The absence of massive royal tombs, palaces and temples, and a clear-cut social differentiation that can be seen in Mesopotamian and Egyptian Civilizations, argues against a centralized state. The distribution of wealth, while not uniform was not very uneven either. The state structure in Harappan cities may have been in the formative stage with ruling councils administering different cities.
- The presence of baths in houses, public wells, bathing areas, high-quality drainage systems speaks highly of the importance given to water and sanitation more than 4000 years back.
- The high level of planning and provision of basic necessities for inhabitants reflects high standards of town planning and humanitarian outlook.

- The sophisticated water conservation system of channels and reservoirs built of stone in Dholavira is the earliest found anywhere in the world.
- The decline of Harappan cities was due to a combination of factors and not due to external invasion.

Fact-check (answers at the back)

1. Harappan cities reached their peak in the mature Harappan phase. (Yes/No)
2. Harappan cities represented the first urban culture in the Indian subcontinent. (Yes/No)
3. Most Harappan cities lacked basic drainage facilities. (Yes/No)
4. Dholavira had a sophisticated water conservation system consisting of channels and reservoirs. (Yes/No)
5. The Harappan cities revealed a huge disparity in wealth and status among citizens. (Yes/No)
6. Typical structures found in Harappan cities (tick right ones):

   a. Fire altars
   b. Citadel
   c. Bathing areas
   d. Public wells
   e. Slaughter houses

CITIES OF THE SECOND PHASE OF URBANIZATION

(600–300 BCE)

WITH THE DECLINE OF THE HARAPPAN CITIES DUE TO VARIOUS FACTORS IN THE LATER PHASE ENDING AROUND 1300 BCE, THERE IS A LONG INTERREGNUM OF STAGNATION AND VILLAGE LIFE. IT IS ONLY AROUND THE SIXTH CENTURY BCE THAT URBAN SETTLEMENTS SLOWLY SPROUTED AGAIN IN THE MIDST OF FORESTS AND VILLAGES.

These cities were not all uniform in architecture, crafts, housing, standard weights and measurements as the Harappan cities. They were different in the kind of functional roles they played, as centres of political control, or as manufacturing hubs for craft production or as trade hubs. Some cities had more than one functionality. The growth of these cities must have been preceded by centuries of agricultural practices leading to a certain food surplus to provide the basis for urban growth.

Starting from small habitations, these urban centres expanded in size, population and spread. Acquisition of craft skills, expansion of trade routes and the emergence of coins accompanied social complexity in the cities. Political leadership, class differentiation and the emergence of the formative state characterized this period.

Cities acquired generic names according to their functionality or size. A town or city with fortifications was called *pura*. The *nagara* was also a fortress or town. The capital of an empire was called the *rajadhani*.

Classification of ancient urban settlements according to the Pali canon	
Pura	Town or city often associated with fortifications
Nagara	Fortress or town
Nigama	A market town, midway between *gama* (village) and *nagara*
Nagaraka	Small town
Mahanagara	Big city
Rajdhani	Capital of an empire

A bigger city became a *mahanagara*. The classification has overlaps since the meaning of the terms differed from region to region.

The growth of cities gave rise to a wide range of occupations such as washermen, tailors, barbers, soldiers, metal smiths, blacksmiths, carpenters, and wage workers. Specialist occupations such as physicians, surgeons, scribes, accountants, and entertainers also flourished. Craftsmen lived in colonies in the cities. The hereditary nature of crafts gave rise to *jatis*. Certain *jatis* enjoyed some upward mobility within the rigid *varna* system. Literary sources confirm the emergence of socio-economic classes, wealth differentiation and concentration in control over productive resources.

> **DEVELOPMENT OF THE JATI SYSTEM**
>
> The growth of cities gave rise to a wide range of occupations. Specialist occupations like physicians and surgeons flourished as well. The heredity nature of the crafts gave birth to *jatis*. Certain *jatis* enjoyed upward mobility in the rigid *varna* system.

Trans-regional trade routes such as the *uttarapatha* in northern India and *dakshinapatha* in central and southern India became arteries of economic activity.

Quite a number of Buddhist, Puranic and Jaina texts help our understanding of the period. A number of Greek and Latin narratives, around Alexander's military expeditions, also throw light on this period.

Nevertheless, there is much less archaeological data available on the cities of this period than those of the Harappan ones. This is because many areas have still not been explored in depth. Moreover, many historical cities have continued to exist till today, making excavations and unearthing the earliest layers difficult. Since it is difficult to separate layers, most archaeological reports present an average picture of the city spread over several centuries. But a redeeming feature is that, unlike the Harappan cities whose history was constructed using only archaeological data, the early historical cities have been described in literary sources as well.

A LITERARY HISTORY OF THE EARLY HISTORICAL CITIES

- The 18 Mahapuranas including Vishnu, Narada, Bhagavata and others.
- The Upapuranas which are many and are secondary Puranas.
- The Dharmashastra texts such as the Manusmriti.
- Buddhist sources such as the Sutta Pitaka, Vinaya Pitaka, Jataka stories and others.
- Jaina canonical and non-canonical works such as the Angas, Puranas, etc.
- The Sangam corpus including *Ettutogaithe*, Eight Anthologies and *Pattupattu* (the Ten Idyls) and epics such as the *Cilappatikāram*.

It should be kept in mind that though urbanization was preceded by agricultural growth and created a food surplus in the entire northern part of the Indian subcontinent, the cities in the region were not products of the same factors everywhere, and they grew at different times and a different pace. Therefore, readers will notice large variations among cities discussed in this section, as compared to the Harappan cities.

Some of the urban settlements such as Rajagriha and Kaushambi could be classified as *mahanagara*. They had fortifcations such as turrets and watchtowers and exhibited the vibrant hustle and bustle of urban life.

Charsada

Charsada has a long history. Referred to as Pushkalavati in the early Indian sources, it is believed traditionally that the city was founded by Puskara, the son of Bharata and the nephew of Rama. Alexander's historians who accompanied him during his invasion in the fourth century BCE mention this city only in passing.

It was Arrian, a later Greek historian, who gives prominence to the city as one which resisted Alexander's invasion and that after subjugation it was put under a Macedonian garrison commanded by Philip.

A BRIEF HISTORY OF CHARSADA

Archaeological deposits found at Charsada, in Bala Hisar, belong to1400 BCE.

Charsada was the capital of the Kingdom of Gandhara from the sixth century BCE to the second century CE.

The city fell into the hands of many rulers such as the Durrani Empire, the Macedonian Empire, the Mauryan Empire, the Indo-Greeks, the Kushans, and the Gupta Empire.

By all accounts the city was very important during the Indo-Greek period. According to the Periplus , it was part of the trade network in which goods from Kabul valley, Kashmir, sub-Hindukush area and those imported from Scythia were transported to Barygaza (modern Broach) on the Narmada River.

The old and the new city

The excavations by John Marshall and Mortimer Wheeler, British archaeologists, related this city to the sixth century BCE, at which time the region was annexed by the Achaemenid. The remains of Charsada are spread over many mounds spanning an area of four square miles. Only two of them seemed to have been planned habitations. At Bala Hisar, the highest mound at the site, archaeologists could unearth a variety of stupas and other buildings.

When Hephaestion, a general in the army of Alexander, seized the city around 327 BCE, the city defences had been strengthened by a ditch and a mud rampart. The ditch enclosed an area of about fifteen acres. The rampart was 4.8 m broad. The habitations of the city spread beyond the enclosed area along a riverbed.

In the other mound of Shaikhan, just 600 metres away, there is evidence of extensive planning.

ALEXANDER'S INVASION OF INDIA

In 326 BCE, Alexander the Great, the king of Macedonia, invaded India, defeating King Porus in the battle of the Hydaspes.

He remained in India for about nineteen months, and returned when his troops, homesick and war weary, refused to go further and forced him to return home.

Find a wall, follow it and pull them out!

> **THE EMPIRE OF THE KUSHANS**
>
> The Kushans ruled between the second century BCE to the third century CE. They were originally from north-western China. Kanishkais the most famous among Kushan emperors.

In the words of Mortimer Wheeler, 'a series of parallel streets – not less than five can be identified – 40 yards apart divide the site into blocks in which coherent house-plans can be isolated. One street-interval, slightly larger (50 yds.), includes the precinct of a massive circular structure which can only have been a stupa or Buddhist (less probably Jaina) shrine. The stupa stood on a slight rise and both by situation and by plan, dominated the scene. But like all the other buildings shown on this very notable air-photograph, it is in negative. It is represented solely by the spoil-trenches dug by the village plunderers, on the principle of 'find a wall and follow it and pull them out, It can be said that the whole site was laid out upon a single co-ordinated rectangular plan, with the temple in its midst.

Just as Takshashila was the old city and Sirkapthe the new city with extensive planning, Charsada seems to be the old city and Shaikhan, the new city. The cities have repeatedly come under the influence

> **THE INDO-GREEK KINGDOM**
>
> Also known as the Yavana Kingdom, the Indo-Greek Kingdom covered parts of modern-day Afghanistan, Pakistan, and northwestern India. They ruled from the second century BCE to the beginning of the century CE first. They were a political entity with a mix of Indian and Greek culture. They are also known as Bactrian Greeks.

> **NORTHERN BLACK POLISHED WARE**
>
> Northern Black Polished Ware (NBPW) is a special type of pottery of urban Iron Age. It is characterized by a glossy surface and was black and red in colour.

of Indo-Greek rulers and the Kushans.

Over the civic plan laid down by the Indo-Greeks, the Kushans built drains, refuse pits and cesspools of a wider street. The houses of this period were of mud brick. In a room, a fireplace was identified 'placed in the middle just in the same fashion as we see in modern Pathan houses.'

A house of the same period belonged to a Buddhist teacher. It had a central open courtyard with rooms on three sides. The fourth side was closed by a high dividing wall. A bathing place, connected by a stone-built drain to the street outside, was situated in the courtyard. It also had a shrine with the figure of Buddha installed in it.

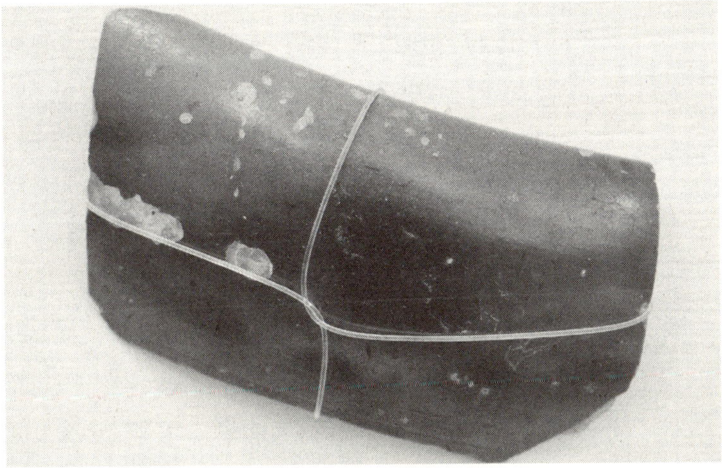

Figure 10: *Fragment of Northern Black Polished Ware*

A timeline of **Mathura**

Sixth century BCE — Mathura became the capital of the Surasena Kingdom.

Fourth to second centuries BCE — Ruled by the Mauryan Empire

Second century BCE — Under indirect control of Shunga dynasty

180–70 BCE — Under the direct or indirect control of the Indo-Greeks

First to second centuries CE — Under the Kushan Empire

300–500 CE — Under the Gupta Empire

Seventh century CE — Under Harsha, the Pushyabhuti emperor

1018 CE — The city was sacked and many of its temples destroyed by Mahmud of Ghazni.

Mathura

Throughout history, Mathura has had an enviable record of serving as the capital for several kingdoms and as an important political centre.

Mathura had its beginnings as early as 1000 BCE, and by the sixth century BCE, Mathura became the capital of the Surasena Kingdom. The city later came under the Mauryan Empire between the fourth and second centuries BCE. Megasthenes, the Ancient Greek historian, writing about India in the early third century BCE, mentions Mathura as a great city.

Beginnings of urbanization

In Mathura, the beginnings of urbanization are discernible between the late fourth to second century BCE. The pottery is related to the NBPW culture. The size of the settlement increased, and a mud fortification wall came up. Coins entered trade. There is considerable evidence of specialized crafts such as the manufacture of terracotta figurines, copper and iron products, and bead-making.

The city may not have played an important role in the Shunga dynasty as the archaeological remains of the dynasty have not been found in Mathura.

From around 180 BCE to 70 BCE, the city may have come under the direct or indirect control of the Indo-Greeks.

After a period of local rule when it was not part of any kingdom, Mathura again fell into the clutches of the Indo-Scythians during the first century BCE, but it was not for long.

Figure 11: *General view of the excavations in January 1889 at Kankali Tila, Mathura*

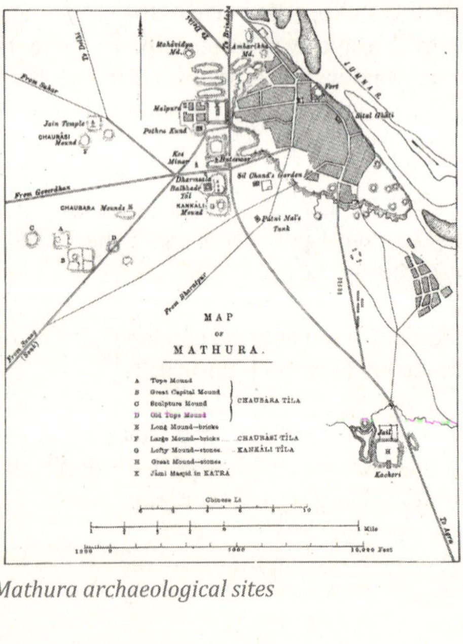

Figure 12: *Mathura archaeological sites*

> **THE GRANARY AT MATHURA**
>
> In 1893, a small inscribed bronze plaque was discovered by an inhabitant of Sohgaura village, presently located in Gorakhpur district of Uttar Pradesh. It was a typical plaque of those times, with a rough surface and holes in the four corners, for fixing on a wall. The short four-line inscription was in the Prakrit language, recorded in Brahmi script. There were seven symbols arranged on top. It was an order issued by the *mahamatras* (officials) of Shravasti (situated in present-day Uttar Pradesh; it is the location where the Buddha gave most of his talks). The contents confirmed that Mathura, along with other cities, served as a storage point for goods, to be distributed to surrounding areas in times of drought. Scholars have not agreed whether it belonged to the pre-Mauryan or post-Mauryan period, the latter being more likely.

Layers of past buried one over the other

Mathura was an important city of early historical India. There are copious literary references to the city from Brahmanical, Buddhist, Jaina and classical sources.

Archaeological explorations were done at many places mentioned in the Mahabharata including Mathura. They have unearthed evidence of a type of pottery called Painted Grey Ware (PGW) that can be dated to as far back as 1000 BCE. They confirm that these sites were inhabited at that time. Archaeological remains also suggest that the

> **PAINTED GREY WARE CULTURE**
>
> Painted grey ware is characterized by a style of fine, grey pottery with geometric patterns in black. It is associated with village and town settlements and probably corresponds to the middle and late Vedic period.

main occupations of the people who lived here were pastoral and agricultural.

The epic Mahabharata and the Puranas associate the city with the Yadava clan, which included the Andhakas and Vrishnis, among whom it is believed that Krishna was born, who later migrated to Dwarka in western India. Mathura city, which has survived until today, stands at the entrance of the fertile Ganga plains. It was an important junction where trade routes meet each other.

The earliest habitation was at the Ambarish Tila, close to the Yamuna, north of Mathura city. It is marked by PGW and shows the gradual growth of a village settlement. Another area, 25 km south-west of Mathura at Sonkh, displays both PGW and Black and Red Ware (BRW) as well as a coarse grey ware. Based on these, the settlement can be dated around 800–400 BCE.

Golden age of sculpture

Under the rule of the Kushans, art and culture reached new heights and survives to this day as the Mathura. Mathura was one of the capitals of the Kushan Empire (second century BCE–third century CE). Ateliers of artists, architects and sculptors in the city buzzed with activity during the reign of Kushan emperors like Kanishka, Huvishka, and Vasudeva – whose reign represents the Golden Age of Mathura sculpture. After the decline of the Kushan Empire, during the third

> **MATHURA SCHOOL OF ART**
>
> - A style of Buddhist visual art that flourished in Mathura from the second century BCE to the twelfth century CE. The art is recognisable for its spotted red sandstone sculptures and statues.
>
> The Mathura style was famed for creating art for the three major religions: Jainism, Buddhism, and Hinduism.

century, Mathura came under the rule of the Nagas.

Much later, during the reign of Chandragupta II, Vikramaditya(380–415 CE), the third ruler of the Gupta Empire, a magnificent temple of Vishnu was built at the site of Katra Keshavadeva in the city.

Around this time, somewhere between 399 and 414 CE, the Chinese monk Fa-Hsien visited India, to study Buddhism, to locate sutras and relics and obtain copies of Buddhist books that were unavailable in China at the time.

Figure 13: *Parkham Yaksha, front and back view*

THE YAKSHA AT MATHURA

Stone and terracotta images of *Yaksha* and *Yakshis*; their female counterparts, have been discovered in the subcontinent, leading to the assumption that they must have been worshipped in many sites. *Yakshas* are deities representing fertility and nature. *Yakshis* are deities connected with fertility.

Among the many *yaksha* images found in the Mathura area, the most celebrated is the imposing grey sandstone figure discovered at Parkham village, which is south of Mathura city. The Brahmi inscription on its pedestal suggests third century BCE, around the period of Ashoka's rule. The inscription gives details of the sculptor. The inscription also indicates that this was an image of the *Yaksha Manibhadra*, a deity worshipped by merchants and travellers.

'The *Parkham Yaksha* gives firm proof of the early use of stone for plastic art and its monographic formula sets it forth as the grand ancestor of subsequent Indian statuary. The free-standing pose carved in the round, colossal size, attitude of the two hands, the right one near the shoulder and the left akimbo, the drapery as an upper scarf and dhoti, the ornaments as torque, triangular necklace, armlets, bangles, bold and gracious expression, majestic stance and impressive volume have been skilfully integrated in a frontal frame which mark the *Parkham Yaksha* as an exemplar in the whole range of historic Indian art' (Vasudeva S. Agrawala, (1965). *Masterpieces of Mathura Sculpture*. Prithivi Prakashan, Varanasi. p. 2.).

The image was removed from Parkham village to the Mathura Museum many years ago. In the month of Magh (January), however, a *Jaikhaiya mela* (i.e. *yaksha* fair) is held where a small *yaksha* image substitutes the original.

Fa-Hsien reported that the people of Mathura were prosperous. He found them peaceful, compassionate towards animals, and conservative in food habits and in consuming liquor. There were no taxes other than for tilling the royal land. According to him, engraved title deeds were issued to landowners. He expressed appreciation that visiting religious leaders were provided with all comforts to pursue their scholarly works.

Later, during the reign of Harshavarshana (606–647 CE), another Chinese traveller, Xuanzhang, visited the city in the year 634. According to him, the city was home to twenty Buddhist monasteries and five Hindu temples.

Hastinapura

Located on the right bank of the River Ganga, the mound of Hastinapura in Meerut district, Uttar Pradesh, was excavated in

> **THE HISTORY OF HASTINAPURA**
>
> Archaeological remains from the Hastinapura site can be dated back to Bronze Age represented by the Ochre Coloured Pottery Culture (OCP). This culture existed during 2000–1500 BCE.
>
> Iron Age culture replaced the Bronze Age culture around 1200 BCE.
>
> During the later Vedic period, painted grey ware culture, which goes back to 1100 BCE, was predominant.
>
> Hastinapura is referred to as the capital of the Kuru Kingdom in the Mahabharata and the Puranas. This perhaps corresponds to the northern black polished ware (600–200 BCE).
>
> In the early 1950s, B.B. Lal, Director General of the ASI, carried out excavations at Hastinapur.

1950–52. Just as many other ancient cities, it had been inhabited over a considerably long stretch of time. The earliest settlement belonged to the period before c. 1200 BCE and the latest level to the early-fiftheenth century CE. Archaeologists have found several layers of settlements corresponding to different cultural, political and economic instances in the life of the city.

The city finds mention in ancient texts such as the Mahabharata and the Puranas as the capital of the Kuru Kingdom. It is also referred to in ancient Jain texts.

According to the epic–Puranic tradition, Hastinapura was the Kuru capital until a flood led to the capital being shifted to Kaushambi. According to the Jaina tradition, the first tirthankara, Rishabha lived in this city, that Mahavira often visited.

Unearthing the cultural layers of Hastinapura

Archaeological findings and literary sources have their own importance in reconstructing the history of a city. When the archaeologist B.B. Lal undertook excavations in Hastinapura in 1952, he tried to correlate his archaeological findings with what was described in the Mahabharata. His excavations unearthed several cultural layers. The cultural layers provided evidence and a brilliant snapshot of the life of the people who lived in the site over the centuries. The earliest was characterized by the ochre coloured pottery. The second layer

> **OCHRE COLOURED POTTERY CULTURE**
>
> A Bronze Age culture of the Indo-Gangetic Plain, generally dated 2000–1500 BCE, extending from eastern Punjab to northeastern Rajasthan and western Uttar Pradesh.
>
> The pottery's distinguishing feature is its ochre colour, that gives it the appearance of being badly fired.

related to the PGW phase of cultural development. Soon thereafter, a flood destroyed the city. After an interregnum, the city was occupied again, this time by people using NBPW and iron implements.

The first of the layers (pre-1200 BCE) came up with a flimsy occupation at the site. Immediately after the Hastinapura findings, the PGW remnants were found in many other sites in Punjab, Uttar Pradesh and Rajasthan. The cultural sequence at Hastinapura turned out to be a very important reference point to reconstruct the history of other sites in the upper Ganga valley.

A brief outline of the cultural layers of

Hastinapura

Period I **1200** BCE	Findings came up with a flimsy occupation at the site.
Period II **1100–800** BCE	This phase revealed the use of PGW pottery. Houses were constructed using mud, mudbrick, reed and mud plaster.
Period III **600–200** BCE	The city was one among the many cities in the region that had the Northern Black Polished warephase.
Period IV **Second to late third century** BCE	The manufacturing techniques had advanced. A number of bowls with curved rims, bottle-necked sprinklers and miniature vases have been found

The second layer represented the period 1100–800 BCE. This phase is important because it revealed the use of PGW pottery. Houses were constructed using mud, mud-brick, reed and mud plaster. Burnt brick may also have been used. However, just the fact that many other sites with similar cultural layers were mentioned in the Mahabharata and that Hastinapura was destroyed by a flood, should not be construed as validating the truth of the story told by the epic. The only fact that the excavations established was that the particular cultural layer found in Hastinapura and other locations coincided with the period in which the epic took place.

During the period 600–200 BCE, called period III, the city was one among the many cities in the region that had the northern black polished ware phase. Archaeologists have revealed an element of planning, burnt-brick structures, and terracotta ring wells in this phase.

During Period III, excavations revealed that burnt bricks of three sizes were generally used for construction of houses, notwithstanding the fact that mud and mud bricks were also resorted to occasionally. There were three structural levels in one cutting and six levels in another. A burnt brick wall, twenty-eight feet long, as well as a room, about fifteen feet square, was traced. Burnt brick drains were in use. These were more likely civic drains, while household drains were vertically placed tall jars with perforations at the bottom serving as soak pits.

Among the excavated terracotta wells, there were two types, one a shallow well with only a few rings; the other much deeper. The first type may have actually been a soakage pit.

The Period III occupation came to an end tragically due to a large-scale fire, evident in the presence of burnt-out remains across the excavated area.

Coming to the archaeological finds belonging to Period IV (second century BCE–late third century CE) we find that the manufacturing techniques had advanced. A number of bowls with curved rims, bottle-necked sprinklers and miniature vases have been found. The pottery had stamped and incised designs such as fish, leaves, flowers and other geometric patterns.

The habitations revealed a certain amount of planning. Seven structural sub-phases were identified for this period. The houses were all made of burnt brick. A ring well was unearthed and a large number of iron and copper artefacts were discovered. Handmade and moulded terracotta figurines, such as the humped bull, showed finesse. Among the finds was a terracotta torso of the bodhisattva Maitreya. The artefacts attested the high quality of workmanship. The discovery of coins of the rulers and Mathura and the Yaudheyas along with imitations of the Kushana king Vasudeva pointed to political alignments.

Takeaways

- From the time the Harappan cities declined, it took a long time until the sixth century BCE for urban revival in north India.
- The cities in this period had several functional roles and did not have the kind of homogeneity in architecture, sculpture, and standard weights and measurements as the Harappan cities.
- Political leadership, class differentiation and the emergence of the formative state characterized this period.
- Quite surprisingly, there is much less archaeological data available on the cities of this period than those of the Harappan ones due to continued existence of these cities till today. But the redeeming feature is that literary sources have contributed to an understanding of these cities in ancient times.
- These cities were important during the Magadhan, Indo-Greek, Kushan and the Gupta periods.

Fact-check (answers at the back)

1. The early historical cities described in this chapter emerged immediately after the decline of the Harappan cities. (Yes/No)

2. Unlike the Harappan cities whose historical reconstruction depended on archaeological findings alone, the story of early historical cities could be reconstructed from archaeological findings, inscriptions, coins and literature. (Yes/No)

3. The cities in this period were alike and had the same functional roles. (Yes/No)

4. There is more archaeological evidence available about the cities of this period than the earlier Harappan cities. (Yes/No)

5. An ancient city has at the most 2 cultural layers. (Yes/No)

6. Hastinapura had a unique type of pottery and houses compared to other cities in this period. (Yes/No)

7. Hastinapura was the capital of:
   a. Panchala Kingdom
   b. Matsya Kingdom
   c. Kuru Kingdom
   d. Surasena Kingdom

8. A *mahanagara* is:
   a. A small habitation
   b. A fortress
   c. A capital
   d. A big city

MAURYAN CITIES

(324–187 BCE)

THE MAURYAS ESTABLISHED AN EMPIRE THAT ENCAPSULATED ALMOST THE WHOLE OF THE INDIAN SUBCONTINENT AND STRETCHED BEYOND IN THE NORTH-WEST. THEY BUILT THEIR EMPIRE ON THE FOUNDATIONS LAID BY THE RULERS OF THE NANDA DYNASTY. THE FIRST THREE MAURYAN RULERS, CHANDRAGUPTA (324–297 BCE), BINDUSARA (297–273 BCE) AND ASHOKA (268–232 BCE) MADE A TREMENDOUS IMPACT ON URBANIZATION IN THE SUBCONTINENT.

The information sources for this period vary immensely; there are a number of literary sources. The Puranas and Jaina works provide a list of Mauryan kings but, unfortunately, they don't tally with each other. Some information can be gleaned from the Buddhist *Mahavamsa,* Patanjali's *Mahabhashya*, and from the poems of the Tamil poet Mamulanar. Among the textual sources for reconstructing this period, Kautilya's *Arthashastra* and Megasthenes' *Indica* have special significance.

The fourth and third centuries BCE witnessed further urban expansion as compared to the previous centuries. Cities expanded and new ones were established in the region that was controlled by the Mauryan Empire.

As cities expanded, there was a significant rise in the specialization in crafts, formation of trade guilds, and use of money in trade transactions. Rising literacy levels and an increasing tendency to put things in writing unleashed a flurry of royal inscriptions being carved on stone. Business transactions were being recorded using a script.

> **THE MAURYAN EMPIRE**
>
> The Mauryan rulers built the first pan-Indian empire. It spanned across central and northern India as well as over parts of modern-day Iran.
>
> Founded by Chandragupta Maurya, the empire was centred at Pataliputra near the junction of the Son and Ganga Rivers.

Compared to the cities covered in the previous section, the ones discussed here are relatively new. Cities like Pataliputra, Takshashila and Ujjaini achieved prominence during the rule of the Mauryan kings. Their excavations revealed cultural layers spanning several centuries. A higher level of political structure, administration, trade networks and guilds set these cities apart from the ones described in the previous chapters.

> **PATALIPUTRA, TAKSHASHILA AND UJJAINI WERE HALLMARKED BY STUNNING AND UNPRECEDENTED SOPHISTICATION.**

After the collapse of Dholavira and other Harappan cities, it is in the Mauryan period, that we again witness monumental stone sculpture and architecture. The development of art and architecture in this period is directly linked to the emergence of a powerful empire, an increase in concentration of wealth with the royal family, ministers, administrators and merchants, and consolidation of religious institutions.

Pataliputra

It was in 1892 when the location of this ancient city was first identified by Laurence Waddell, a military officer. Excavations in the early twentieth century near the modern city of Patna revealed the remnants of large fortification walls reinforced by wooden trusses.

> **WATER FORT**
>
> Water Fort is a type of fort surrounded by water bodies that could either be natural (sea or rivers) or artificial (moats, artificial lakes). For example, the Murud-Janjira Fort in Maharashtra is surrounded by the Arabian Sea on all sides.

The city had its beginnings as a modest fort originally built by the Magadha (South Bihar today) ruler Ajatashatru in 490 BCE near the Ganga River. This place was then called Pataligrama. His son and successor Udayin laid the foundation of the ancient city at the confluence of the Ganga and Son Rivers. After realising the importance of the central location of the city, Udayin moved his capital from Rajgriha to this city.

This is confirmed in Buddhist sources that mention that a city was being built towards the end of the Buddha's life. This tallies with archaeological evidence showing evidence of urban life in the third or fourth century BCE. Jain and Hindu documentary sources identify Udayabhadra (also known as Udayin) as the king who first established Pataliputra as the capital of Magadha.

As time passed, the city grew in importance and served as the capital for several empires in succession. Pataliputra was the capital of the Shishunaga Empire (413–345 BCE), the Nanda Empire (460–325 BCE), the Mauryan Empire (320–180 BCE), the Gupta Empire (320–550 CE), and the Pala Empire (750–1200 CE).

With its vantage position at the confluence of the Ganga, Gandhaka and Son Rivers, Pataliputra formed a 'water fort, or jaldurga'. This enabled the city to dominate the riverine trade of the Indo-Gangetic plains from Magadha's early imperial period and even later. Pataliputra was a renowned centre of trade and commerce and attracted merchants and intellectuals, like Kautilya, from all over India.

The city also provided with fertile ground for the flourishing of several religious sects. Early Buddhist texts have recorded that two important early Buddhist councils were held here. While the first session of the second Buddhist Council was held in Vaishali, the second session of the second Buddhist Council in the reign of Ashoka, held 35 years after the first session, was conducted here. Later, the third Buddhist Council also took place in this city.

The Sangam Tamil epic *Akananūṟu* mentions the Nanda kings ruling Pataliputra, after Magadha rule.

The jewel of the Mauryan Empire

It was during the Mauryan Empire that the city reached its peak as one of the largest cities of the world, if not the largest. About 305 BCE, Alexander's General, Seleucus Nicator, waged a war against Chandragupta Maurya to recover the territories that Alexander had conquered. He lost badly and peace was concluded by a matrimonial alliance. Seleucus sent an ambassador, Megasthenes, to reside at the Mauryan capital of Pataliputra. He wrote a detailed account of India, including the Mauryan capital. Unfortunately, his manuscripts did not survive, but they could be reconstructed from the writings of many Greek and Latin authors who had quoted him.

IT WAS DURING THE RULE OF SHER SHAH SURI (1538–45) THAT PATALIPUTRA GOT ITS MODERN NAME, PATNA.

PATALIPUTRA DECODED BY THE GREEK DOCUMENTORS

Greek ambassador, Megasthenes, resided in the city and left a detailed account of its splendour, referring to it as 'Palibothra':

'Megasthenes says that on one side where it is longest this city extends ten miles in length, and that its breadth is one and three-quarter miles; that the city has been surrounded with a ditch in breadth 600 feet, and in depth 45 feet; and that its wall has 570 towers and 64 gates.' – *The Indica of Arrian,* translated and annotated by Watson McCrindle, 1876.

'The greatest city in India is that which is called Palimbothra (Pataliputra)... the inhabited part of it stretched on either side to an extreme length of eighty stadia, and that its breadth was fifteen stadia (183 m), and that a ditch encompassed it all round, which was six plethra (186 m) in breadth and thirty cubits in depth; and that the wall was crowned with five hundred and seventy towers and had four-and sixty gates.' – McGrindle, J.W. 1877. *Ancient India as described by Megasthenes and Arrian; being a translation of the fragments of the Indica of Megasthenes collected by Dr Schwanbeck, and of the first part of the Indica of Arrian*. London: Trubner and Co.

Strabo (63 BCE–24 CE), a Greek geographer, philosopher, and historian adds that the city walls were made of wood. These are thought to be the wooden palisades identified during the excavation of Patna.

'At the confluence of the Ganga and of another river is situated Palibothra, in length 80, and in breadth 15 stadia. It is in the shape of a parallelogram, surrounded by a wooden wall pierced with openings through which arrows may be discharged. In front is a ditch, which serves the purpose of defence and of a sewer for the city.' –*The Geography of Strabo with An English Translation By Horace Leonard Jones*, Book XV, chapter 1.

A timeline of **Pataliputra**

1300 BCE — Ruins dating from the Early Harappan period around 1300 BCE were discovered in the site.

1000 BCE — By 1000 BCE, the site had settled inhabitants. It was the capital of the Gandhara Kingdom around 600 BCE.

515 BCE — Emperor Darius, of the Persian Achaemenid Empire, captured Takshashila in 515 BCE.

326 BCE — Alexander the Great invaded the city in 326 BCE.

303 BCE — The city came under the rule of Chandragupta Maurya of the Mauryan Empire in 303 BCE.

Ashoka, the grandson of Chandragupta, made the city a great seat of Buddhist learning.

The Indo-Greeks captured the city in the second century BCE and built a new capital called Sirkap, the twin city of Takshashila.

The Kushans occupied the city in the first century CE.

The Gupta Empire occupied the city in the mid fourthcentury CE.

The Greek traveller and diplomat praised the city as among the first cities in the world to have a highly efficient form of local self-government. According to him, the capital was a magnificent city, surrounded by a wooden wall. An administrative board of thirty members controlled the city. The social and economic life of the people was greatly regulated.

Megasthenes described that the city was enclosed by a wooden wall with towers and openings for archers. A moat surrounded the city for further protection. His account is supported by archaeological evidence in some key aspects. He also reported on the existence of caste, but his classification that the population was divided into seven endogamous groups is a misconception.

Figure 14: Mauryan remains of a wooden palisade discovered at the Bulandi Bagh site of Pataliputra

The discovery of ancient ruins

Ancient ruins related to the capital city of the Mauryan period have been discovered in modern Patna. At Kumrahar, there are remnants of a pillared hall with ten rows of eight pillars each. At another location, in Bulandibagh, remains of a wooden fortification comprising two parallel walls were discovered. It is not clear however, whether they correspond to the wooden fortifications narrated by Megasthenes. In addition, a large wooden drain, a large wooden chariot wheel with spokes and an iron rim, and the foundation of a wooden jetty lying along the old course of the Son River have also been unearthed.

At Kumrahar in Patna, Waddell discovered a pillar fragment in 1903. In 1912–13, D.B. Spooner discovered seventy-two pillars arranged in rows and columns and after a considerable gap, in 1959, A.S. Altekar and V.K. Misra discovered eight more, thus making it a total of eighty pillar fragments.

They were constructed using buff-coloured Chunar sandstone and displayed a polished, smooth surface. They were thinner and shorter than the famous free-standing Asokan pillars. All of them had a hole on top suggesting that they may have been attached to a capital at the top. The presence of a large quantity of ash and burnt wood indicate that the floor and roof were made of wood and had been destroyed by fire. Wooden platforms with a wooden staircase might have formed a passage to the pillars. It is also suggested that a canal might have connected the pillars to the Son River.

Takshashila

Takshashila, an ancient city famous for its world-class university, is located in present-day north-western Pakistan. Excavations at Bhir mound in Takshashila have revealed the presence of habitations in the third century BCE and have shed light on the fact that the city was not constructed according to plan.

Blocks of houses within four streets and five lanes were discovered. A broad 6.7 m wide street coursed through the city, while other streets were narrower and winding. Traces of covered drains could be found. Use of round refuse bins in streets suggested an amount of importance given to sanitation. Houses were protected from traffic in the streets by rough stone pillars in corners. Houses had with rooms around a stone-paved courtyard. Some larger houses had two courtyards. Bathing areas and passages were also paved with stone. The sewage from houses emptied out through stone surface drains and earthen-ware drainpipes connected to soak pits.

A religious complex was also discovered, 60 x 23 square metres in size, with a lane cutting across dividing the structure into a larger northern block and a smaller southern one. The northern block consisted of as many as thirty rooms around two courtyards. A large pillared hall was also seen in the complex. A number of broken terracotta male and female figures were found, perhaps, they were cult images used by devotees.

> **WHO WERE THE GRECO-BACTRIANS?**
>
> The term Greco-Bactrian refers to a Greek kingdom (250–145 BCE) spread over Bactria (Afghanistan) and Sogdiana (the Central Asian region of Uzbekistan and Tajikistan). The region was part of the Seleucid Empire until the Bactrian governor Diodotus declared independence in 250 BCE.
>
> Sogdiana broke away from Bactria around 200 BCE. The kingdom lost its remaining regions to nomadic tribes of Indo-Scythians and Yuezhi around 145 BCE.

The tale of two cities

When excavations took place at the site of Takshashila, two cities were discovered. One of them was built at the time of the Achaemenid kings of Persia. And the other around the Greco-Bactrian period. The two cities stood on either side of a broad street. Houses had a central courtyard, a traditional design from the days of the Harappa culture.

But the cities differed in big ways. As we read earlier, the first city, called the Bhir Mound, showed scant planning. Its streets were not straight and ran into a maze of narrow alleys. Perhaps private builders were active in the city following no rules.

The second city, called Sirkap, however, had a decent main street 20 feet wide, running north to south. Side roads branched off at right angles from the main road. The city layout revealed strict planning. It should be kept in mind that the neat planning of Sirkap

> **THE JANDIAL TEMPLE**
>
> The Jandial temple is an ancient temple well-known for its Greek-style architecture and Ionic columns.
>
> John Marshal of the ASI excavated the temple in 1912–1913.
>
> However, inside the temple, the presence of a heavy wall with a staircase has given rise to the view that it may have been a Zoroastrian temple, built by the Indo-Parthians in the first century BCE, to practise their faith.

cannot be attributed to the Greeks alone, since Harappan cities much earlier had been built very methodically. The new city must have been the creation of a powerful king who wished to build a totally new city rather than setting right the chaos of an existing one.

The temple of Jandial, excavated from one of the mounds which covered the city of Takshashila, is a landmark in temple architecture. The temple had a square inner sanctuary, a meeting hall, and a courtyard. Both its outer and inner sanctuary were flanked by two large pillars designed in the orthodox Ionian pattern. The Jandial temple is believed to have Zoroastrian influence.

Excavations at the site have also uncovered fine jewellery with semi-precious stones set in gold filigree, resembling Indian jewellery of the modern times.

A city claimed by many rulers

In the early sixth century BCE, Takshashila was under the control of the king of Gandhara, who in turn was a vassal of Darius I, the third of the Achaemenid emperors. Young men from Magadha enrolled as students in the university. It is reported that the Magadhan emperor Bimbisara was in contact with Pushkarasarin, the king of Gandhara.

In 326 BCE, the king of Takshashila, Ambhi, submitted to Alexander and the entire city was annexed without resistance. It is said that Alexander was impressed by the austerity of the naked ascetics whom he met at Takshashila.

> **WHO WAS DARIUS I?**
>
> Darius I, also known as Darius the Great, was an Achaemenid ruler known for his administrative genius, his great building projects and his benevolence towards the diverse people in his sovereignty.

When Chandragupta overthrew the Nandas, who were rulers of Magadha, he also subdued the north-west and drove out the Greek garrisons. With that, Takshashila came under the rule of the Mauryans.

After the decline of the Mauryan Empire, the city probably came under the control of the Sungas and later under the Indo-Greeks.

Takshashila, a centre of learning

Takshashila was renowned for its learned teachers and achieved a reputation comparable to that of the university cities of medieval Europe in its heyday. The university was already renowned at the time of the Buddha. But unlike Varanasi, the university here laid more emphasis on secular studies. The Buddhist Jataka tales reveal that young students from all parts of India flocked to this

> Some renowned students of
>
> **Takshashila**
>
> **PANINI** — The famous grammarian.
>
> **KAUTILYA** — The powerful minister at the court of Chandragupta Maurya
>
> **CHARAKA** — Ancient Indian physician and scholar.

city for education. And it is through the university that Iranian and Mesopotamian influence trickled into India. It produced students who later became renowned throughout the world, such as Panini, the grammarian who lived in the fourth century BCE, Kautilya, who became the influential minister at the court of Chandragupta Maurya and authored the *Arthashastra*, the science of statecraft. Charaka, one of the great masters of Indian medical science was also a distinguished student.

The university departed from the traditional Indian Gurukul system of learning, where a small number of students study under a single teacher, called the guru, living with and serving the teacher. Students paid fees and there is a Jataka story that talks about a teacher who gave first preference to paid students, making others wait. The university also allowed married students to live in their own quarters and visit the teachers for lectures.

Sanchi

In the same manner as many other ancient cities and monuments, the relics at Sanchi were in a state of abandonment until a British officer, General Henry Tailor, chanced upon the site in 1818. The site was breached and ravaged by many amateur archaeologists until Sir John Marshall of the ASI took over and restored the structures between 1912 and 1918 and a site museum was set up housing all the recovered antiquities.

But some of the bone relics of Buddhist saints were ferreted out of the country by Charles Maisey and J.D. Cunningham as personal trophies and colonial loot and even sold to museums. However, both of them had contributed immensely to the documentation of the relics at the site. Both the French and British colonialists were keen to take away some mementos from the site to be displayed in their countries in museums.

In spite of protests, many relics are abroad. The Gupta era statue of Padmapaniis is at the Victoria and Albert Museum in London. One of the Yakshini statue resides at the British Museum.

All said and done the monuments in Sanchi have survived the

The Ochre Coloured Pottery (OCP) culture

The Ochre Coloured Pottery culture (OCP) is a Bronze Age culture which prevailed in the Indo-Gangetic Plain, covering northeastern Rajasthan, eastern Punjab, and western Uttar Pradesh. It is found both in the Late Harappan culture and the Vedic culture. It is generally dated 2000–1500 BCE.

Black and Red Ware (BRW) culture

Black and Red Ware culture (BRW) is a late Bronze Age and early Iron Age culture. It was prevalent in the northern and central Indian subcontinent. It is generally associated with the Vedic civilization. It existed from 1450–1200 BCE in the western Ganga plain. In the Central and Eastern Ganga plain and Central India, it extends until 700–500 BCE.

The Painted Grey Ware (PGW)

The Painted Grey Ware (PWG) culture is an Iron Age culture. It was prevalent in the western Gangetic plain and the Ghaggar-Hakra valley. It can be roughly dated from 1200 BCE to 600 BCE. This corresponds to the middle and late Vedic period, when the Kuru-Panchala kingdoms existed.

Northern Black Polished Ware (NBPW) culture

Northern Black Polished Ware (NBPW) is an urban Iron Age culture. It existed during 700–200 BCE. It peaked during the period of the 16 republics, or mahajanapadas, in northern India and the subsequent consolidation of the Mauryan Empire.

A timeline of Sanchi

- **268–238 BCE** — Ashokan period
- **185–73 BCE** — Shunga period
- **First century BCE to Second century CE** — Satavahana period
- **Fourth century -Sixth century CE**

ravages of time fairly well. It is an important tourist and religious site today, well-connected by rail and road. The site caters to both the archaeological enthusiasts and connoisseurs of ancient sculpture.

Though Sanchi is revered as an important Buddhist site, it is not associated with any particular event in the Buddha's life. During the Mauryan period, it won a lot of attention because Ashoka's influential queen, Devi, was born here.

The monuments at Sanchi provide remarkable clues about ancient and medieval India over a period of 15 years to historians. Its lifelike artefacts give us a glimpse into what Indian city life would have been during that period.

Stupa No. 1

Sanchi, predominantly a religious centre, was well-connected with other cities and must have had its fair share of economic activities. There are a number of monuments existing at the site today built over several centuries by many powerful empires. From the Mauryan Empire in the third century BCE to the Gupta Empire of the fifth century CE, embellishments of the monuments continued till the twelfth century.

> **INSCRIPTIONS OF HISTORICAL SIGNIFICANCE**
>
> Structures in Sanchi, especially Stupa 1, have a number of Brahmi inscriptions on their walls. The inscriptions are related to contributions but provide information about the donors in society.
>
> The inscriptions were deciphered by James Princep, a British scholar, who had also done pioneering work in deciphering the Kharosthi script.
>
> Analysis of the list of donors informs us of the close connection between Sanchi and surrounding towns and cities and influential sections of society who donated large sums to the monasteries.
>
> The donors were from cities and capitals such as Ujjaini and Vidisha. Among the donors were a few Greeks too.

Among the monuments, the foremost and the largest structure is the iconic Great Stupa called Stupa No. 1. It was erected during the Mauryan Empire. One of the famous Ashoka pillars was also installed at this time. After the demise of the Mauryan Empire, during the rule of the Shungas and Satavahanas, the Great Stupa was embellished with gates and balustrades. A number of smaller stupas came up in the vicinity. A number of temple structures were also commissioned in the intervening years. It can be said that the monuments at Sanchi represent the evolution and glory of ancient Indian architecture and ancient Buddhist architecture.

A stupa is essentially a monument erected over a burial place. In most ancient civilizations it was customary to protect the remains of important members of society after their death. Usually a circular railing is built around the burial place and the bone relics themselves are preserved under a wooden or a stone monument. Relic worship was introduced into Buddhism only in the third century BCE.

The construction of the stupas is usually characterized by a dome surrounded by a circumambulatory path made of stone. Two flights of stairs led up to the stupa. Stone railings were erected at the base. A stone umbrella sat on the summit of the dome. The entire structure was enclosed by stone railings and four gateways (toranas).

The brick core of Stupa No. 1 belongs to the period of Ashoka. During the Shunga period this Stupa was encased in dark purple-grey sandstone.

The Great Stupa 'is architecturally an eccentric rather than a successful achievement but this does not distract from the fact that it is a most remarkable and interesting structure' . The stupa is not truly hemispherical. What stands out in the structure is that the engravings in the balustrades and gateways should have been executed on wood by a carpenter rather than on stone by a mason. The triple umbrella on top of the stone dome enclosed within a square fence is also a departure from similar structures in other sites.

The balustrades and gateways are decorated with crowded detailed pictures, scenes from the Jataka stories depicting the adventures of Buddha in his numerous previous incarnations and incidents in his life and that of his disciples. Even for a lay visitor the images will be fascinating. There are numerous friezes of war scenes, animals, snake-gods, elephants and chariots and so on. A point of interest is that in Sanchi one cannot find a real image of Buddha but only his representation in the form of a pair of footprints or a tree. The

THE SANCHI STUPA HAS WON SUCH AN EXALTED PLACE IN INDIAN HISTORY AND CULTURE THAT THE RESERVE BANK OF INDIA INTRODUCED INDIAN 200 RUPEE NOTES IN COMMEMORATION OFTHE SANCHI STUPA IN 2017.

friezes are so elaborate and intricate that they must have been worked on by a large number of craftsmen from nearby cities such as Vidisha. But visitors knowledgeable of the style will be able to discern variations in individual workmanship in treating the same theme. Even though these are Buddhist stupas, the products are certainly the work of secular craftsmen who would have been as adept at sculpting images on gateways of shrines as in creating the interiors of a prince's palace.

Temple 40 is the only important structure which was built in Mauryan times along with Stupa No. 1.

During the later Shunga period, as already mentioned, the Stupa No. 1 was enlarged and reinforced with stone slabs to almost twice its original size. The dome was flattened near the top and on it were erected the parasols within a square railing. It is generally believed that Stupa No. 2 and 3 were erected during the rule of the Shungas. But the intricately decorated gateways were done only during the later Satavahana period.

The Satavahanas built the decorated gateways around the stupas built earlier in the Mauryan and Shunga periods. It appears that the balustrade and the gateways were also coloured. The structures belonging to the Satavahana period include pillared halls and shrines. Recent excavations have thrown up evidence of water harvesting and storage for both drinking and agriculture.

During the following Gupta period, several pillars and temples were built.

WHILE NO BONE RELICS WERE FOUND IN STUPA NO. 1, STUPA NO. 2 (WHICH LIES AWAY FROM THE MAIN GROUP OF STUPAS) AND STUPA NO. 3 YIELDED RELICS OF BONE FRAGMENTS OF A FEW FAMOUS BUDDHIST MONKS.

Ujjaini

Ujjayini (modern Ujjain), located on the banks of the Shipra River, a tributary of the Chambal, was the capital of Avanti in the fourth and fifth centuries BCE. It was a major commercial hub, an important junction in the main highways crisscrossing the subcontinent, the *uttarapatha* and the *dakshinapatha*.

Like other cities in the region, Ujjaini has four cultural phases. The earliest, Period I had remnants of BRW and PGW pottery, placing its date around 750–500 BCE. The settlement was protected by an imposing mud fortification wall, surrounded by a moat.

In the second period, we see structures made of mud, mud-brick, and burnt brick. A large burnt brick tank for water storage and several terracotta ring wells were unearthed. Even the remains of an iron-smelting furnace and evidence of manufacturing of stone beads and bone arrowheads were detected.

In the third period, a large number of objects made of iron, terracotta, ivory, and copper have surfaced.

The region has been rich in iron ores and once the art of smelting iron ore using bellows was mastered, the production of iron products proliferated adding an edge both to agriculture and war. The large-scale use of iron made Avanti a formidable opponent to the Magadhan Empire.

Politically, Ujjaini and Pataliputra were on opposite sides since the kingdoms of Avanti and Magadha were at war with each other. Avanti's king, Chanda Pradyota Mahasena, fought Magadha's Bimbisara, but eventually the two worked out a peace treaty. Later, when Pradyota was afflicted by jaundice, it is said that Bimbisara sent the royal physician Jivaka to Ujjain.

WHILE DIGGING FOR SCULPTURAL FRAGMENTS, ARCHAEOLOGISTS CAME ACROSS SEVERAL IRON TOOLS, POTSHERDS AND BOWLS. THE POTTERY HAD A BRILLIANT, ALMOST METALLIC, BLACK POLISHED SURFACE. THIS CAN BE DATED TO THIRD-FOURTH CENTURY BCE. SUCH POTSHERDS HAVE BEEN DISCOVERED IN MANY OTHER SITES IN NORTH INDIA ATTESTING TO THE UNIFORMITY OF PRODUCTS OVER LARGE TERRITORIES IN THE MAURYAN EMPIRE.

A city of major importance

Ujjaini remained the capital of the formidable Avanti when Bimbisara's son Ajatashatru and later Ajatashatru's son Udayin ruled Magadha. Finally when the Shishunagas came to power after Udayin, they destroyed the power of Avanti and temporarily moved their capital to Vaishali. This finally ended the 100-year-old rivalry between Magadha and Avanti. And, from then, Avanti was absorbed into the Magadhan Empire and continued to be so till the end of Maurya rule. Ujjain's status as a capital of a powerful kingdom ended. But it served as the capital of the Western province of the empire during the time of Ashoka. Earlier, during the reign of his father Bindusara, Ashoka served as the viceroy of Ujjayini, which underscored the importance of the town. According to the Sinhalese Buddhist tradition, Ashoka's children Mahendra and Sanghamitra, who preached Buddhism in modern Sri Lanka, were born in Ujjain. Ujjain remained an important city of the Guptas during the fourth and the fifth centuries.

Just like other cities of the period, besides being a political capital, Ujjain also developed into a manufacturing hub and a trading centre. There were guilds of smiths, carpenters, leather workers and other artisans and craftsmen. Workers lived in specific streets and quarters. Specialization in crafts developed to a high level.

Generally crafts were hereditary, and handed over from father to son. Ujjain was connected to other cities by highways. Merchants transported the finished products over long distances. It is said that sometimes, a caravan of five hundred cartloads of goods moved together.

Traders from the kingdoms of Magadha and Koshala travelled up to Mathura and then southward to Ujjain. The city was also connected to southern markets.

Full-fledged urbanization had set in by the time of Alexander's invasion. It is estimated that around 300 BCE, there were 270,000 people living in Pataliputra, 60,000 in Mathura and 38,000 in Ujjain. This kind of population had not been witnessed since the decline of the Harappan cities.

Urbanization fuelled trade, gave rise to a strong state, and ushered in reading and writing. Harappans had a script, so writing must have emerged before the time of the Buddha. However, unfortunately, the earliest records have been destroyed because they were written on perishable material.

Poets heap praise

Many classical poets have praised the city in their works. Kalidasa, the great Indian classical poet of the fifth century who lived in the times of the Gupta king Vikramaditya, lauds the richness of Ujjain and its people in his epic poem *Meghadoota*. In the sixth century, the Chinese pilgrim Xuanzang, who visited Ujjaini, describes the ruler of Avanti as a king who was generous to the poor and presented them with gifts. Bharthrahari is said to have wriiten his great epics in the city. Bhasa, the celebrated Indian playwright who wrote in Sanskrit, lived in Ujjaini and his writings are probably set in the city. The famous play, *Mrichchhakatika* by Shudraka, is also set in Ujjain.

Ujjain was looted several times by the Arabs of the Umayyad Caliphate in the eighth century CE.

Takeaways

- The Mauryas established their empire on the foundations laid by the Nanda Empire.
- The information sources for this period are more varied than the earlier periods.
- There was further expansion during this period accompanied by specialization in crafts.
- The Mauryan cities had a higher level of political structure, administration, and trade networks.
- Pataliputra, the capital of the Mauryan Empire, was one of the largest cities of the world at that time.
- The city of Takshahila in the northwest had a world-class university.
- Ujjayini was an important city in the Mauryan Empire due to its rich iron ores.

Fact-check (answers at the back)

1. The Mauryans built their empire on the foundations laid by the Nanda dynasty. (Yes/No)

2. Ujjayini was the capital of:
   a. Avanti
   b. Magadha
   c. Chedi
   d. Kosala

3. Full-fledged urbanization had set in by the time of Alexander's invasion in the Gangetic plain. (Yes/No)

4. The city of Takshashila was renowned for its:
   a. Parks
   b. Monasteries
   c. University
   d. Rivers

5. After the Harappan cities, it is only at the time of the Mauryan cities that we witness monumental stone sculpture and architectures. (Yes/No)

6. Who among the following was not a student of Takshashila university?
   a. Panini
   b. Ajatashatru
   c. Kautilya
   d. Charaka

7. Bhir mound and Sirkap are two parts of Takshashila. (Yes/No)

SANGAM CITIES

(400 BCE–300 CE)

The earlier view was that the cities of the far south came up much later than those of the Indo-Gangetic Plains in the North. However, recent archaeological data from sites such as Kodumanal have pushed the date to at least the fourth century BCE. The early kingdoms of the region known as Tamilagam, roughly comprising the area between the Tirupati Hills and Kanyakumari, flourished around riverbeds. The Cholas ruled the lower Kaveri belt, with their cities in modern Thanjavur and Trichinopoly districts. Their capital was situated at Uraiyur. The Pandyas ruled the region south of the Kaveri, watered by the Tamiraparani and Vaigai Rivers, covering present-day Madurai, Ramanathapuram, Tirunelveli districts, and southern Kerala. The Cheras, who controlled the western coast of Kerala, had their capital at Karuvur, also known as Vanji, and going by the name of Karur today.

> **THREE CROWNED KINGS**
>
> **The Cholas:** One of the longest-ruling dynasties in the world, with its capital at Uraiyur
>
> **The Pandyas:** Also referred to as the Pandyas of Madurai, difficult to establish their origin and timeline
>
> **The Cheras:** Credited as the 'Creators of the land of Kerala', they unified various regions of the western coast and the Western Ghats

All these kingdoms were served by busy ports; Puhar

being the main Chola port, Korkai serving the Pandyas, while Tondi and Muchiri enabled sea trade for the Cheras.

The Sangam poems provide a good description of the cities. However, one must keep in mind that a lot of these poems are often exaggerated since they were sung to praise the valour of kings or to display emotions of love. Thankfully, the Tamil-Brahmi inscriptions come to the rescue by providing the chronology of kings and chieftains, and both of these sources can be compared to gather more information. The kings were called *vendar* and the chieftains who paid tribute to them were called *velir*. The three kingdoms were always at war with each other, each forming shifting alliances.

Inscriptions throw evidence on administration and merchant guilds. A second-century BCE inscription recovered in Mangulam mentions a *kalatika*, an officer who supervised pearl fisheries. He was also a member of a merchant guild. Another inscription from Alagarmalai,, belonging to the first century BCE, refers to a *kanatikan*, the chief of scribes. Such inscriptions clearly indicate an advanced level of administration, trade and literacy.

Urbanization in Sangam cities: Nascent or advanced?

Some historians have characterized the urbanization in this period as nascent, with the region still ruled by tribal chieftains who had control just over the area they ruled and were primarily dependant on plunder and tributes from other areas. But the presence of a highly developed Sangam literature, urban centres specialising

SOME SANGAM POEMS, VERY FEW THOUGH, WERE ALSO ON RELIGIOUS THEMES. PARIPADAL IS A PRIME EXAMPLE THAT HAS POEMS ABOUT VISHNU, SHIVA, DURGA AND MURUGAN.

in crafts, and flourishing external trade point to the existence of a sophisticated structure in state and administration. Trade in gold, gems, wine, horses, and muslins establish that cities served as manufacturing hubs and trade centres. Trade in luxury goods point to wealth differentiation in urban centres. Coins were used in trade, indicating advanced form of financial transactions.

Along with the exchange of trade goods, there was also an intermingling of religious ideas and philosophies during this period. Buddhism and Jainism penetrated the South as well, and Vedic sacrifices and worship of puranic deities showed effect on local cults and deities. Rituals, sacrifices, and patronage of ascetics became the new bases for royal legitimacy.

Greek and Roman sources mention many cities that they called emporiums. Several ports called *pattinam* in Tamil existed along the eastern and western coasts. While Sangam poems mention many towns, archaeological excavations have not yet confirmed all of them. Since many ancient cities have been continuously occupied till now, further excavations are not possible.

Sangam kingdoms and sea trade

Figure 15: *This multi-text palm leaf manuscript (UVSL 589) with 100 folios, handwritten in miniature scripts by Shaiva Hindus, includes many Tamil texts, including the Sangam era Tirumurukāṟṟuppaṭai*

EMPTYING THE ROMAN TREASURY

When Gaius Petronius Arbiter, a Roman courtier under Nero, chided fashionable Roman ladies for exposing their charms much too immodestly by clothing themselves in the 'webs of woven wind', referring to the fine muslins imported from India, it wasn't the lone complaint of a paranoid protectionist. Pliny the Elder was more vehement when he remarked 'this is the price we pay for our luxuries and our women'. Their agitation was well-founded. Indian cities reportedly drained the Roman Empire annually to the extent of fifty-five million sesterces – around half a million pounds – sending in return goods which were sold there at a hundred times their value in India. By the time of Augustus, one hundred and twenty ships were setting sail every year from Myos Hormos to Indian ports. This meant that as far back as the first century of the Common Era, Indian cities and ports were powerhouses of world trade.

The *Periplus* of the Erithraen Sea talks about South Indian ports such as Musiri, Korkai, Kaveripattinam, Kodumanal, and Arikkamedu. Poets eulogised 'Musiri to which come the well-rigged ships of the Yavanas (then a term for the Romans and which later also included the Greeks), bringing gold and taking away spices in exchange'. The air in these ports was redolent of vibrant cosmopolitanism, more variegated than anywhere else in the subcontinent. Since the Indian ports exported much more to Rome than they imported, trade was almost one-sided. Roman gold coins were hoarded in the cities, if not melted, building a huge external balance.

The Tamil kings, driven by the requirements of external trade, did much to develop harbours and encourage sea trade. Sangam literature talks about lighthouses and wharves where 'the beautiful great ships of the Yavanas' discharged their merchandise. The port was manned by customs officials, who stamped the merchandise with the king's seal and despatched them to storehouses.

Vanji

Vanji, also called Karuvur, was the capital of the Chera dynasty. Today the city is known as Karur and is situated along the banks of the Amaravati, a tributary of the Kaveri River. Home to eleven Sangam poets, the city's status as an important political centre as well as a manufacturing and trading hub is confirmed by literary and archaeological findings and supplemented by evidence gleaned from inscriptions and coins.

The treasure unearthed

Excavations have revealed BRW potsherds with graffiti marks, locally made rouletted ware and even pieces of Roman amphorae, which are tall jars presumably used to transport and store wine. In and around the city, Roman coins have been discovered in large quantities, some from the time of the Roman Emperor Claudius of the first century CE. Copper coins bearing Chera symbols, such as the bow and arrow, were also found, giving the clue that a mint might have been located in the region. Literary sources confirm that jewel making was an important craft practised in the city, confirmed by the discovery of finger rings. Tamil-Brahmi inscriptions unearthed near the city narrate donations made by Chera rulers as well as craftsmen and merchants, indicating the existence of an elite and the tradition of giving donations for religious activities.

The mention of the Vani River flowing near the Chera capital shows that Karuvur was in fact Vanji. The discovery of Chera inscriptions near Karur and of thousands of Roman coins in Karur and its neighbourhood and Ptolemy's statement that the inland city of Korura was the Chera capital also point to the same conclusion. The recent archaeological excavations at this site, especially the find of Roman amphorae pieces, conclusively prove the identity of modern Karur with the Vanji of the Sangam age.

It is assumed that around the third century CE, the city must have passed its peak of prosperity and political power. A poet called Nattattanar describes in one of the ten idylls that charity had dried up in the capitals of the three Tamil kingdoms and all the ancient patrons of learning and the arts have disappeared!

Several inscriptions were unearthed in places like Pugalur and Arachchalur, in the vicinity of Karur, along a trade highway, which are records of gifts to Buddhist or Jaina sects by the Chera ruling family and elites of the kingdom such as rich merchants and craftsmasters. They indicate the influence that monks of the sramanic religions wielded among the ruling class and mercantile classes in the South as far back as those days. This also indicates a certain amount of upward mobility for the non-Brahmin castes and jatis. Evidence of a large gem and jewel manufacturing centre in Kodumanal, a city situated nearby, points to Vanji's importance as a commercial and trading centre.

Royal patronage to sramanic sects

The Tamil epics written after the Sangam anthologies testify to the fact that Vanji was a large urban complex with many Buddhist and Jain establishments. The epic *Manimekalai* refers to a *chaitya* in the city, built by the predecessor of Kovalan. The hero of another epic, *Silapathikaram*, became a monk after donating all his wealth to a monastery. At Vanji, an Indra vihara is also said to have been constructed on the lines of another vihara at the port city of Puhar. The existence of such viharas in key cities of the Tamil region in that period indicates that Buddhist establishments were close to urban centres, usually situated in their outskirts. While later tradition has tried to place their dates at the time of Ashoka, these establishments must have been built in the early centuries of the millennium by merchants and trade guilds.

Muchiri (Muziris)

While Vanji was the capital of the Chera dynasty, Muchiri was its premier port. According to the *Periplus*, ships from Arabia and Egypt set anchor near the port waiting for their goods to be unloaded. However, Pliny contradicts this statement a little by saying that due to danger of the pirates, ships dropped their anchor at a safe distance from the port. But wherever the ships were set at anchor, it can't be contested that a large number of goods were imported and exported from here.

The exact location of Muziris is still being debated among historians

ROMAN NATURALIST PLINY ON MUZIRIS

Roman naturalist Pliny the Elder (23 to 79 CE) wrote about his voyages to India in the first century CE. He refers to many Indian ports one among which is Muziris. However, by the time he visited the port city, it may not have been a favoured location in Roman trade on the western coast of India. In his words:

'If the wind called Hippalus (south-west monsoon) happens to be blowing, it is possible to arrive in forty days at the nearest market in India, Muziris by name. This, however, is not a very desirable place for disembarkation, on account of the pirates which frequent its vicinity, where they occupy a place called Nutrias; nor, in fact, is it very rich in articles of merchandise. Besides, the road stead for shipping is a considerable distance from the shore, and the cargoes have to be conveyed in boats, either for loading or discharging. At the moment that I am writing these pages, the name of the King of this place is Celebothras'. (Pliny the Elder. 1855. *The Natural History*, Translated By John Bostock, and H.T. Riley, Vol. II , Book VI, P. 65)

and archaeologists. However, some evidence has been found from excavations since 2004. It is believed that Pattanam, near North Paravur, a suburb of Kochi, is the location of the ancient city.

A favoured port for maritime trade

A second-century document called the Vienna Papyrus describes an agreement related to the transportation of goods between two merchants, one based in Alexandria and the other in Muziris.

In 2020, a seal ring with the carving of the Sphinx, which looks similar to the one worn by the Roman Emperor Augustus Caesar about 2,000 years ago, was discovered at Pattanam. This reiterates the description of the city in Greco-Roman and Sangam sources that Muziris was a centre for flourishing trade in goods. And that it connected the countries of the Greco-Romans, the Egyptians, the West Asians, the Africans, the South Arabians, the Indians, and the Chinese. They also point to the substantial maritime commercial, technological and cultural exchanges between Eastern Mediterranean and ancient Tamilakam.

> **THE LOCATION OF MUZIRIS**
>
> Muziris, an ancient harbour and an important trading port on the malabar coast, finds its mention in Sangam literature and in other classical sources. While the exact location is still not known, Pattanam in Kerala is thought to be where the city was located.

Madurai

Ancient Madurai, considered as the 'Athens of South India' because of its cultural significance, was the capital of the Pandya Kingdom. Madurai is, till today, one of the largest cities of Tamil Nadu.

> **CAPTIVATING DESCRIPTIONS OF MUZIRIS**
>
> The *Akananuru*, an anthology of early Sangam poems, provides an exciting description of Muziris:
>
> *The Pandyan king leading mighty elephants,*
> *with great din besieged the prosperous Chera town of*
> *Musiri where, stirring white foams on the lovely Periyar river,*
> *ply the beautiful ships of the Yavanas,*
> *which come bearing gold and depart with pepper.*
>
> (Ettuthogai – 149.7-11) (Translation by author)

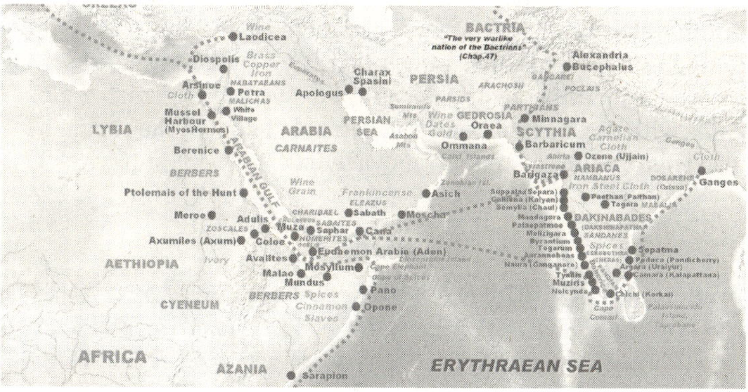

Figure 16: Indo-Roman trade relations

Maduraikanchi, one of the Ten Idylls, describes it as a prosperous and large city sitting on the banks of the Vaigai River, with other three sides enclosed by walls. Tamil tradition states that this city was the place where the third Sangam was held. The poem describes the city's mansions, markets, festivals, and people in beautiful poetry. The city was also the second major location in the epic *Silapathikaram*, describing the story of Kovalan and Kannagi, after Puhar port.

Since Madurai has had a continuous settlement from ancient times, it has been impossible to carry out archaeological excavations in the occupied parts. But those conducted in the surrounding regions provided significant and extensive enormous information on the political, cultural and economic life of the region.

Tales excavation findings tell

Tamil-Brahmi inscriptions as early as the sixth century BCE have been found in Keeladi. Other sites such as Alagarmalai and Mangulam have also shown useful findings. Roman coins have been found in the region, some of them in the city itself. A hoard of silver punch-marked coins have been unearthed from Bodinayakanur, a site nearby. They display a double carp symbol on the reverse and other punch marks on the obverse side. They have been identified with the Pandya dynasty. Other square copper coins with the elephant and fish symbols found in the region have also been attributed to the Pandya dynasty.

THE TAMIL EPIC SILAPPATHIKARAM RELATES THE STORY OF YOUNG MERCHANT KOVALAN LIVING IN THE PORT CITY OF PUHAR. HE IS MARRIED TO THE VIRTUOUS KANNAGI. BUT HE FALLS FOR THE COURTESAN MATAVI, RESULTING IN HIS RUIN AND EXILE TO MADURAI. THERE, WHEN HE TRIES TO SELL HIS WIFE'S ANKLET, HE IS MISTAKEN FOR STEALING THE QUEEN'S ANKLET AND PUT TO DEATH. KANNAGI ON HEARING OF HIS DEATH, GETS AN AUDIENCE WITH THE KING AND PROVES KOVALAN'S INNOCENCE. IN GRIEF AND ANGER, SHE CUTS OFF ONE BREAST AND THROWS IT AT THE CITY, WHICH GOES UP IN FLAMES ILLUSTRATING THE POWER OF INNOCENCE.

IDYLLIC 'MADURAIKANCHI' ON THE CITY OF MADURAI

'Maduraikanchi' is the longest of the Ten Idylls. The poet Mangudi Maruthanar describes the city in chaste poetry. Sharing some translated passages from his poem:

The city walls are sky-high and contain strong sally-ports and gateways old and strong on whose door posts is carved great Lakshmi's form. Their strong-built doors are blackened by the ghee Poured as libation. And above the gates Are rooms that look as high as loudcapped hills, Through which pass streams of men like the Vaigai's flow. The houses there have rooms of diverse kinds That seem to reach the skies and windows broad Through which the south wind blows. In wide long streets That are as broad as rivers, crowds of folk Of various professions and speech create a noise in the morning market-place while buying things. The loudly-beating drum which makes a noise Like the wind-swept ocean's roar announces loud To all a festival. When instruments Are played with ease, as one runs one's hands In water, those who hear their music dance With glee and shout, in streets where morn and eve The people buy and sell. The streets present a very charming scene. There one may see the various pennons used at festivals; those flags of victory great with various names, presented to the chiefs who took day after day fort after fort...

(Source: *Chelliah, J.V. Pattupattu: Ten Tamil Idylls.* P. 177–178)

Trade on one hand, manufacturing on the other

Madurai was both a manufacturing and trading hub. The city's artisans specialised in gold ornaments, ivory work, inlay work, chank cutting, and bangle making. There are references to trade in pearls and precious stones. As early as the second century BCE, the *Arthashastra* describes Madurai as a centre of fine cotton textiles.

Figure 17: Eighth-century Thirupparankundram cave temple, Madurai

Excavations have unearthed a horde of coins, including ones issued by the Pandyas. Early Tamil–Brahmi inscriptions have been found at sites near the city indicating a level of commercial activity and literacy. Inscriptions dug up from a place called Alagarmalai record endowments made by merchants from Madurai.

> **THE OLDEST CITY OF TAMIL NADU**
>
> Madurai is probably the oldest city of Tamil Nadu and has been ruled by the Pandyas, Cholas, Madurai sultanates, Vijayanagara Empire Marathas, and British East India Company.

According to a story, 12,000 Jaina disciples migrated to the South along with their teacher Bhadrabahu and Chandragupa Maurya, who had also taken the vow as a Jain monk. They settled in Sravana Belagola in Karnataka and went further south. They found

Madurai and its surroundings ideal for living a secluded life and for following their practices. To date, at least fourteen such caves around Madurai have been located. These caves consist of carved, polished rock beds, and other facilities to live a frugal life. In these rock caverns, one can find early Tamil (Tamil-Brahmi) inscriptions that might be dated between 500 BCE to 300 CE. The earliest among them was discovered at Mankulam village that has five natural caves and six inscriptions.

Kaveripumpattinam (Puhar)

Puhar was, in the ancient times, a flourishing ancient port city under the rule of the Cholas. Located near the mouth of the Kaveri River on the eastern coast of Tamilagam, the port city finds mention in the Sangam period Tamil poem 'Paṭṭiṉappālai'. The poem devotes two hundred and ninety-six lines of three hundred and one to the description of this port in the period of the Chola king Karikalan. Besides this poem, the epics *Silappadhikaram* and *Manimekalai*, and the poem 'Akananooru' also throw light on this ancient port.

When we piece together archaeological and literary evidence, it is possible to get some idea of the economic development of the city at that time. We find mentions of the specialized crafts like metal working, bead making, and weaving. The descriptions available in *Pattinapalai* of the markets of Puhar, the references to the elite sections of the city, and the mention of use of money—all these things attest to a certain level of economic development and social stratification in South India even in that period.

The port city today

The city is now a decaying fishing village; its harbour destroyed by silt, but in the Sangam era, it had an artificial harbour, built by soldiers captured by King Karikalan in a raid on Lanka.

It has been established beyond doubt by marine archaeological research under the leadership of K.V. Soundararajan that much of the town was washed away by the erosion of sea and massive floods. Marine archaeologists have, in recent times, excavated submerged wharves and considerable lengths of pier walls. And archaeological remains of pottery have been found in the site dating back to the fourth century BCE, proving the corroborations to the literary references to Puhar.

> **THE ANCIENT PORT CITY**
>
> Puhar was once a flourishing ancient port city that finds description in Sangam literature as the capital of the early Chola kings. However, much of the town was washed away by regular floods and erosion.

Two faces of a town

The Tamil epic *Silapadhikaram* reveals that the port town had two districts, Maruvurpakkam facing the sea and Pattinappakkam to its west. These two districts were separated by a patch of gardens and orchards where daily markets were held under the shade of trees. The markets functioned twenty-four hours; the day market was named Naalangadi and the night market was called Allanmgadi.

Maruvurpakkam, located near the shipyard, had terraced mansions and warehouses. There were quarters for fisherfolk, silk merchants, weavers, potters, grain merchants, and jewellers. Overseas merchants and travellers, going by the general name of *yavanas*, set up temporary or permanent homes in the city.

While Maruvurpakkam was inhabited by the working people, traders, and seafarers, Pattinapakkam was the elite section of the city, where the royalty, elite traders, professionals, army officers, and court dancers lived.

HOW PAṬṬIṈAPPĀLAI DESCRIBES PUHAR

The Paṭṭiṉappālai, one of the Ten Idylls, describes Puhar in exotic poetry. Though it gives an idealised description of merchants plying their trade, it is informative. Here are some verses:

In the upper floors of mansions, women with pretty feet, close thighs, wide loins, coral-like bodies covered with fine fabric, delicate appearances like peacocks, deer-like bewildered glances and parrot-like sweet language, wear new jewels, and stand near doors through which breezes blow. Their stacks of bangles are like the beautiful petals of drooping clusters of glory lily blossoms that drop fine pollen in the tall mountains. In the sweet Puhār harbour, desirable flags are hoisted on masts of ships gently swaying on the waves, anchored and appearing like male elephants that sway their sturdy posts.
The borders of the city with great fame are protected by the celestials. Swift horses with lifted heads arrive on ships from abroad, sacks of black pepper arrive from inland by wagons, gold comes from northern mountains, sandalwood and akil wood come from the western mountains, and materials come from the Ganga. Pearls come from the southern ocean and coral comes from the eastern ocean. The yields of river Kāveri, things from Eelam, products made in Burma, and many rare and big things are piled up together on the wide streets, bending the land under.

Archaeological remains have been found in many villages nearby attesting to a number of habitations around the port city. There are remains of an artificial channel that drew water from the Kaveri into a reservoir for irrigation purposes, probably built in the early centuries of the first millennium. The port city had brick platforms for landing boats. The presence of a Buddhist temple and monastery built around the third century points to the influence of Buddhism in that period. The discovery of early medieval Chola coins in the site indicates that the port continued to thrive during the reign of the Cholas as well, between the ninth and twelfth centuries.

Keeladi

During the course of its investigations, the Archaeological Survey of India revealed a Sangam era settlement, located 12 km southeast of Madurai in Tamil Nadu. The settlement revealed two hundred and ninety-three sites all along the Vaigai River valley and carbon dating revealed that the samples sent were about 2,200 years old. Many urn burials, menhirs, inscriptions, and sculptures were unearthed during the course of its investigations. Among these, the Keeladi site which stretched to 110 acres was the most promising as cultural deposits in the area showed that a large habitation had once thrived here.

Figure 18: *Archaeological remains and artefacts of Keeladi*

Figure 19: *Pot found in Keeladi, providing proof of Vaigai River Civilization*

Thousands of antiquities were unearthed. One type of finding involved structural materials such as brick structures, terracotta ring wells, and roof structures. The other type was related to gold ornaments, copper objects, iron implements, terracotta toys, semi-precious stones, and more.

CHESS, A CULT FAVOURITE EVEN IN BYGONE ERA

It appears that chess was popular among people living in ancient cities as far back as 2600 years!

In the historic period, gamesmen (chess pieces) were made of terracotta or ivory. Excavations at Keeladi have unearthed both hopscotches and gamesmen. The majority of the gamesman recovered are of terracotta. As many as six hundred hopscotches were unearthed. Even today, the game of hopscotch, called *pandi* in the local language, is popular in Tamil Nadu.

A number of dice were recovered from the site. Around eighty similarly shaped chessmen, but in different sizes, were also found.

Figure 20: Archaeological remains and artefacts of Keeladi

The pottery found here were of several types such as black and red ware, black ware, black polished ware, red ware, and rouletted ware.

Several Tamil-Brahmi inscriptions were also found. From all these materials, we can assume that there was once a large and culturally developed habitation near the ancient city of Madurai.

The interesting fact is that these archaeological samples fall between the sixth century BCE and the third century CE. And since there are deposits below the lowest cultural layer unearthed so far, one can safely assume that Keeladi was a flourishing city even in sixth century BCE.

South India at par with North in urbanization

The findings at Keeladi have led to a reappraisal of the general theory offered so far that urbanization in South India started much later than in the north. If the sprawling city had existed in the sixth century BCE, then historically, it is as relevant as the ancient cities of Mathura and Ayodhya. The presence of large-scale brick structures and the high-value products excavated confirm that the second urbanization which occurred in the Gangetic plains from the sixth century, also extended to the Tamil region.

For example, earlier excavations in places like Kodumanal and Alagankulam fixed the date of the invention of the Tamil-Brahmi script at around the fifth century. But recent discoveries of inscriptions in Keeladi written in Tamil-Brahmi have pushed the date back at least by one century, if not more. Such evidence helps to draw the conclusion that urbanization in Tamilagam might have started at the same time as that of the Gangetic plains.

Takeaways

- Urbanization in Tamilagam started around the same period as in the Gangetic plains. There is enough evidence to establish that cities and ports were hubs for internal and external trade and that a certain level of state structure, administration, trade, and literacy existed.
- The cities and ports served the three major kingdoms of the Cholas, Pandyas, and Cheras.
- The two ports described in this chapter, Puhar and Muziris were linked to trade networks extending to Africa, Arabia, Egypt, and the South-east.
- Increase in manufacture and trade was accompanied by wealth differentiation with the poorer and richer sections living in separate parts of the cities.
- Colonies of craftsmen and trade guilds sprung up in cities.

Fact-check (answers at the back)

1. Urbanization in Tamilagam started much later than that in the Gangetic Plain. (Yes/No)

2. Tribal chieftains ruled the region surviving on war booty and tributes. (Yes/No)

3. The state was non-existent or in its formative stage in the Sangam period. (Yes/No)

4. Urbanization in the south started many centuries after that in the Gangetic plains. (Yes/No)

5. Puhar had a day market and a night market. (Yes/No)

6. Which dynasty among the following did not rule a part of the Tamil area during the Sangam period?
   a. Chera
   b. Chalukya
   c. Chola
   d. Pandya

7. Which of the cities below was not a capital of Sangam dynasties?
   a. Madurai
   b. Thanjavur
   c. Badami
   d. Karur

EARLY CITIES OF THE DECCAN

(SECOND CENTURY BCE–SIXTH CENTURY CE)

After the decline of the Mauryan Empire, numerous small kingdoms sprouted in the Deccan, until the advent of the Satavahanas, who united the region. The Satavahanas go by the name of Andhras in the Puranas. However, there is some vagueness regarding their chronology. Some coins discovered in this region name the rulers that are not present in the Puranas. The rule of this dynasty began in the second century BCE and ended in the early third century. At its height, the Satavahana Empire covered modern Andhra Pradesh and Maharashtra, and also included northern Karnataka, eastern and southern Madhya Pradesh, and Saurashtra. According to Pliny, the region had many

Major dynasties that ruled the

Deccan region

Satavahanas	Late second century BCE to early third century CE
Vakatakas	Late second century BCE to early third century CE
Western Chalukyas	543–757 CE
Eastern Chalukyas	624–1070 CE
Rashtrakutas	753–982 CE
Yadavas	1187–1317 CE
Kakatiyas	1163–1323 CE
Vijayanagara	1336–1646 CE
Bahmani Sultanate	1347–1527 CE
Deccan Sultanate	1490–1686 CE
Marathas	1674–1818 CE

villages, thirty walled towns, a large army of 100,000 infantry, 2,000 cavalry and 1,000 elephants.

The Shakas and Satavahanas were always at loggerheads over the control of ports in the region such as Bhrigukachcha (Broach), Kalyan and Suparaka (Sopara).

Textual references are not available on the early cities of the Deccan, so their history has been reconstructed on the basis of archaeology alone. The cities of the Deccan have always been under the shadow of the Mauryan empire and Indo-Roman trade. Even within the Deccan there is a lot more information on places where Ashoka's inscriptions or Buddhist structures exist than the rest of the region.

After the decline of the Satavahanas, the Deccan came under the rule of the Vakatakas, the Chalukyas of Badami, the Western and Eastern Chaulkyas and the Rashtrakutas. Each of them left their imprint on the cities of the Deccan.

Religious tolerance was one of the hallmarks of the ancient and early medieval Deccan cities. Buddhism and Jainism flourished along with Vedic practices. The cities are repositories of some of the most exquisite sculptures and paintings in the Indian subcontinent.

Nagarjunakonda

The historical city of Nagarjunakonda now lies buried under the lake created by the Nagarjuna Sagar Dam. But fortunately the archaeological relics were excavated and transferred to a higher land. The city's remains were first discovered in 1926 by the French archaeologist Gabriel Jouveau-Dubreuil.

In the 1950s when the decision was taken to construct the Nagarjuna Sagar Dam, a large number of relics dating from the Early Stone Age to the sixteenth century were excavated and transferred to a museum on the Nagarjunakonda hill. Other sculptures were transferred to museums in Delhi, Chennai, Kolkata, Paris and New York.

Nagarjunakonda was home to a Buddhist monastic complex which attracted students from far away places like China, Gandhara and Lanka. Ruins of several Buddhist and Hindu shrines have been excavated. Other reliefs of antique times having a Roman influence have also been found. The city once known by the name of Vijayapuri took on its modern name after a southern Indian master of Mahayana Buddhism who lived in the second century.

Coins and inscriptions discovered at the site establish that Buddhism had spread to the region by the time the Satavahana king Gautamiputra Satakarni came to power.

Figure 21: *Buddha Statue discovered in the ruins of Nagarjunakonda*

But it was towards the early third century CE, after the decline of the Satavahanas and the rise of the Ikshvaku dynasty (225–340 CE), that the city rose to prominence. The Ikshvakus made the city their capital. They constructed several temples and Buddhist monuments. During the early centuries of the first millennium the city housed more than thirty Buddhist viharas. Besides Buddhist stupas and relics, there are also Saivite shrines and temples

> **THE AMARAVATI SCHOOL OF ART**
>
> Amaravati is the most important site for a well-known regional style called the Amaravati school, or style, of art.
>
> The style is characterized by crowded scenes. Each scene depicts a number of graceful figures who display a vigorous sense of life and action.
>
> The sculptures are embellished with decorative elements. The figures are deep cut so that their overlapping is possible. The bodies of the human figures are superlatively sculpted and they stand in a variety of poses. Together they display a swirling motion of a mass of figures. The entire surface of the art panels is filled with figures in motion.

dedicated to Karthikeya. The findings of Roman coins suggest trade relations with the Roman world. It is believed that the Ikshvaku kings had employed a garrison of Scythian guards in the city.

After the fall of the Ikshvakus, the city lost its prominence, It was much later, during the fifteenth and sixteenth centuries that the city again came into the limelight. The Reddi rulers built a frontier fortress at the site. It later came under the control of the Gajapatis and subsequently, the Vijayanagara king Krishnadeva Raya captured the city when he defeated the Gajapatis.

Amaravati (Dhanyakataka)

Generally believed to be the site of ancient Dhanyakataka, which was an important town in the Deccan and according to many inscriptions, the capital of the later Satavahanas, Amaravati is a major site in Guntur district. The city was an influential centre of Buddhism. Despite rising to prominence in the medieval period, it had ancient roots. Six occupational periods have been discovered after excavations extending from the second century BCE to the second or third century CE. Inscriptional evidence suggests that

Figure 22: *Life scenes of Buddha found in Amaravati*

the origins of the Buddhist establishment may be as early as the Mauryan period.

The ancient city had a citadel that was surrounded by a massive mud fortification. Soak-pits and drains were discovered in the remains. Since remnants of a navigational channel and an impressively large wharf were discovered, it can be assumed that the city had maritime connections. Both of these were discovered to be repeatedly renovated in various phases of occupation. Ancient artefacts included a goldsmith's mould, glass bangles, and a variety of earrings.

The Amaravati stupa was among the largest in the subcontinent in those times and is referred to in ancient inscriptions as a *mahachaitya*. Unfortunately, very little of the original structure has survived till today.

The art of Amaravati

When the Satavahana dynasty reached its zenith in the second to third century CE, the Amaravati stupa was enhanced with limestone reliefs depicting scenes of the Buddha's life and surrounded by his figures. These reliefs are among the greatest works of Indian art. They convey an intense vitality, quite unexpected in the context of a religion that preaches peace and control of the senses. Particularly the relief showing a host of joyous demi-gods carrying Buddha's begging bowl to heaven depicts vigorous action, bordering frenzy. The Amaravati school of art had a profound influence on Lankan, South-east Asian, and South Indian sculpture. Today Amaravati is the capital of the state of Andhra Pradesh.

Ajanta

The very name Ajanta conjures up a vision of rock-cut caves in the middle of sylvan surroundings, where Buddhist monks could pursue their religious duties without getting distracted by the world outside. True to the vision conjured, the Ajanta caves have been cut out of the rolling hills of the Maharashtra plateau. The Wahora streamlet tumbles down along a precipitous cliff. The caves have been havens for exquisitely chiselled sculpture and masterly renditions of paintings. If one could get a bird's-eye view, one would see a semi-circular scarping along the hillsides and the caves themselves are visible as dark recesses bored into the rock.

There is no documentation on Ajanta until the account given by the Chinese pilgrim Xuanzang, who visited India in the first half of the seventh century, and was so attracted to what he saw that he decided to stay on for fifteen years. However, although he did not visit Ajanta, he managed managed to write an interesting account from available documentation at that time.

The site was thereafter neglected for centuries until 1819, when officers of the Madras Army chanced upon the caves. It took some more years for a serious study. In 1843, James Ferguson presented the importance of the rock-cut 'temples' to the Royal Asiatic Society. He was the first one to give a chronological and architectural perspective to the caves.

Figure 23: *Ajanta caves near Aurangabad*

In 1871, Fergusson and James Burgess of the Archaeological Survey of India conducted fresh surveys, scrutinising the architectural details of the caves, deciphering inscriptions, and figuring out the political period as well as the subjects of the paintings. Since the paintings had deteriorated over time, efforts were made to copy the paintings with fidelity and also capture them through colour photography.

THE DISCOVERY OF AJANTA CAVES

1819: A chance discovery by British soldiers on a hunt.

1843: James Ferguson, Scottish architectural historian, presented accounts of the caves to the Royal Asiatic Society.

1871: Fresh surveys were conducted to figure out the subject, political period, and inscriptions of the caves.

1956–1957: Countless people through the years tried to copy the murals. In 1956, this task was taken up by the ASI and authentic copies of the murals were made.

1983: The Ajanta caves were declared a UNESCO World Heritage Site.

A well-connected centre

Though Ajanta could be called a religious centre, its location in the midst of arterial trade routes may indicate that it could have been visited by traders, government officers, and others and served as a resting place for pilgrims and merchants. It is just 130 kms away from Paithan (Pratishthana), the capital of the early Satavahanas. It is also not far away from the arterial route connecting the northern cities to the South, through Ujjain and Mahishmati – which are on the Dakshinapatha. It is also quite close to Amaravati and Bhokardan. And it must have also been connected to the western port of Barygaza (today's Bharuch). The recessed caves, the sound of the tumbling waterfalls, the chirping of birds, chattering monkeys, water-laden clouds, and the quietness of the hills must have been a great attraction to visitors. Or at least, this is the description we get from inscriptions in the caves.

> **AJANTA CAVES**
>
> The Ajanta caves are considered masterpieces of Buddhist religious art. The paintings paintings and sculptures at Ajanta present an important specimen of art; architecture; socio-cultural, religious, and political history of the contemporary society. The caves together house the largest repository of ancient Indian paintings.

It is not just Ajanta, but a number of nearby sites in western Deccan are also repositories of Buddhist monasteries, worship halls, paintings, and sculpture. The question arises, why did the Buddhist monks select this region for building their network of monasteries? Perhaps the fact that Ashoka (273–36 BCE) sent emissaries to Sopara, a flourishing port town nearby, to create his rock edicts must have been the inspiration behind choosing this place to build the monasteries. The perpendicular cliffs and the surrounding forests and rivers provided the ideal conditions to excavate the rock caves and set up monasteries. Their choice has proven correct since the caves have endured the ravages of time. It is not a wonder that out of an estimated twelve hundred rock-cut excavations, eight hundred are situated in west Deccan.

The Ajanta Caves and their significance

The twenty-nine rock-cut Buddhist cave monuments in the Ajanta Caves date from the second century BCE to about 480 CE. The caves are located in Aurangabad district of Maharashtra. The rock-cut sculptures and paintings are among the finest surviving specimens of ancient Indian art and sculpture. The paintings, particularly, exude intricate emotions through a variety of gestures, poses, and forms.

The caves were built in two phases with a gap of a few centuries between them. Five of the caves belong to the Satavahana period, while the remaining belong to the later Vakataka period. Of these two caves are *chaityas* 41 and the rest are *viharas* 42. The Satavahanas had their capital in Pratishthana. Though they believed in Vedic orthodoxy, they encouraged Buddhism as well. They brought political stability to the Deccan and promoted trade and commerce with West Asia. About five to six centuries after the fall of the Satavahanas, Ajanta began humming with activity again. This time the patronage came from the Vakataka rulers; who,are a testament to the idea that without patronage from royalty and elites they could not have been excavated. According to the well-known art historian Walter Spink, Cave 1 is 'the most sumptuous rock-cut *vihara* ever made in India'. The cave was built at the time of Harishena (480–510 CE), the Vakataka ruler. The *chaityas* and the *viharas* have been carved into a 75-metre wall of rock. The paintings in the caves describe the past lives and rebirths of the Buddha, rock-cut sculptures of Buddhist deities, and pictorial tales from the Jatakas. The caves together house the largest repository of ancient Indian paintings.

Today, the site is a protected monument in the care of the Archaeological Survey of India, and since 1983, the Ajanta Caves have been a UNESCO World Heritage Site.

Figure 24: *Inside view of Ajanta Cave*

Takeaways

- The Deccan Plateau of the Indian subcontinent is located between the Western Ghats and the Eastern Ghats and is bounded by the Narmada River in the south and the Satpura and Vindhya Ranges in the north.
- The region produced some of the major dynasties in Indian history, including the Pallavas, Satavahanas, Vakatakas, Chalukyas, and Rashtrakutas, along with the Western Chalukya Empire, the Kadambas, the Yadava dynasty, the Kakatiya Empire, the Vijayanagara and the Maratha empires.The Bahmani and Deccan Sultanates were from of the Deccan Plateau too.
- The history of the Deccan starts in the second century BCE with the establishment of the Satavahana dynasty, which brought political stability to the region.
- After the decline of the Satavahanas, the Deccan came under the rule of the Vakatakas, the Chalukyas of Badami, the Western and Eastern Chaulkyas, and the Rashtrakutas.
- Deccan has been a centre of Buddhist activity since the time of Ashoka, when he sent emissaries to the region.
- Pratishthana, the capital of the Satavahanas, lay on the radial artery connecting the northern cities with the South.
- Rulers and elites of the Deccan provided patronage to Hindu, Buddhist, and Jain temples and monasteries.

Fact-check (answers at the back)

1. The Deccan is bounded by the Narmada River in the south and the Vindhya Ranges in the north. (Yes/No)

2. The Ajanta caves were built in a single phase. (Yes/No)

3. The elite of Deccan patronised all religions. (Yes/No)

4. The cities of the Deccan are only religious centres and not commercial centres. (Yes/No)

5. Out of twelve hundred rock-cut excavations in the Indian subcontinent, eight hundred are situated in the Deccan. (Yes/No)

6. The history of Deccan starts from the sixth century CE. (Yes/No)

7. Amaravati has both Buddhist monasteries and Hindu temples. (Yes/No)

8. Which Chinese traveller documented Ajanta:
   a. Faxian
   b. Xuanzang
   c. Song Yun
   d. Yijing

9. Nagarjunakonda now lies buried under a lake. (Yes/No)

CAPITALS OF THE PALLAVAS, CHALUKYAS AND PANDYAS

(600–900 CE)

FROM THE SIXTH CE TO THE NINTH CE, THE DECCAN AND SOUTH INDIA WERE DOMINATED BY THREE POWERS, CONSTANTLY AT WAR WITH EACH OTHER AND SEEKING TO EXPAND THEIR EMPIRES AT THE COST OF OTHERS. THEY WERE THE CHALUKYAS OF BADAMI, THE PALLAVAS OF KANCHIPURAM, AND THE PANDYAS OF MADURAI. AS MANUFACTURING AND TRADE INCREASED, THEIR CAPITALS WERE ABUZZ WITH ACTIVITY. BY THE EIGHTH CENTURY, THE CHALUKYAS OF BADAMI WERE WEAKENED AND THEIR PLACE WAS USURPED BY THE RASHTRAKUTAS OF MANYAKHETA (MALKHED). BESIDES HAVING THEIR HEADQUARTERS AT BADAMI, THE CHALUKYAS BRANCHED OUT INTO THE WESTERN CHALUKYAS WITH THEIR CAPITAL AT KALYANI AND THE EASTERN CHALUKYAS WITH THEIR SEAT OF POWER IN VENGI. IN BETWEEN, CAME THE GANGAS OF MYSORE. MADURAI WAS THE OLDEST OF THESE CITIES, ITS EXISTENCE RECORDED FROM THE SANGAM PERIOD.

MAJOR DYNASTIES

THE PALLAVAS

Early fourth century to late ninth century rulers who played a major role in shaping the history and culture of South India. They rose to prominence after the downfall of the Satavahana dynasty.

THE CHALUKYAS

Classical Indian dynasty that ruled large parts of southern and central India between the sixth and 12th centuries.

THE PANDYAS

Celebrated in the earliest Tamil poetry, the Pandyas were amongst the ancient Tamil dynasty of South India that faced decline and upliftment periodically.

Political conflict, however, did not come in the way of growth of the cities. And, under the stimulus of the Bhakti movement, temple architecture advanced in these cities.

Besides serving as centres of general administration, the capitals also served as residences of the royalty. This section deals with Kanchipuram and Badami. We have already described Madurai in an earlier section.

Kanchipuram

There are references to Kanchipuram by the Sanskrit grammarian Patanjali, as early as the third century BCE. The fourth century poet Kalidasa described the city as 'the best among the cities'. The city is also widely regarded as the Benares of the south. Sangam literature like the epic *Manimegalai* mentions the city.

Kanchipuram, situated on the north bank of the Vegavati River, a tributary of the Palar River, had an early start as the capital of a pre-Pallavan chief by the name of Tondaiman Ilanthiraiyan. The city was surrounded by a tall rampart and protected by a deep moat. Only from the beginning of the fourth century, did it become the capital of the rising Pallavas and remained so till the nineteenth century. Once the imperial Cholas defeated the Pallavas, the city became a secondary capital.

BHAKTI SAINTS AND THEIR POETRY

The Tamil bhakti saints employed different styles of verses in their poetry.

'Pathigam' is a poem in praise of a deity usually consisting of ten stanzas.

'Pasuram' is a song of praise addressed to a deity usually sung by the Vaishnavite Alwars.

Treasure trove of cultural experiences

During this period, the city kept expanding to meet the needs of a capital – a mercantile centre and a religious centre. Buddhist viharas, Jaina pallis, and Saivite and Vaishnavite temples thrived in the city. Xuanzang, who visited the city in 634 CE, confirmed the existence of several Buddhist viharas. The city was home to several Buddhist monks and scholars. Both Dinnaga, founder of Buddhist logic who lived in the early sixth century, and Dharmapala, a well-known commentator of Buddhist texts who lived in the seventh century, had made the city their home.

The greatest architectural masterpiece of Rajasimha Pallava (690–728 CE), in fact, of the entire Pallava dynasty, is the Kailasanatha temple at Kanchipuram. Inside the temple, there are fifty-eight miniature shrines in the compound wall encircling the sanctum and the mandapa in front. Some of the shrines still retain traces of paintings in pleasing colours, its outlines barely visible and almost in complete state of deterioration. The temple boasts of elegant sculptures created in soft stone, the majority of them depicting Siva in his various forms.

The city is famed for being a centre of Sanskrit education, the *Ghatika,* which is said to have attracted the founder of the Kadamba dynasty, Mayurasarman, to pursue Vedic studies in 350 CE.

In the post-Sangam period, when there was an impetus to urbanization, Kanchipuram rose to the status of a *nagaram*, a mercantile centre. With the ascension of the Pallavas, the city became their capital.

Kanchipuram had trade connections with China from as far back as the second century BCE. The Chinese writer Ban Gu, who lived in the first century CE, refers to trade ties with Kanchipuram.

Figure 25: *Kailasanathar temple in Kanchipuram*

Threat from the world outside

Kanchipuram functioned as a hub for manufacturing, trade, culture, and spirituality. It was also a city that constantly faced external threat. Therefore the Pallavas fortified the city with ramparts and wide moats. During the reign of the Pallava King Mahendravarman I, the Chalukya King Pulakesin II (610–642) laid siege to the capital city. The Pallavas, however, successfully thwarted the Chalukya siege and foiled their repeated attempts to capture the city. In retaliation, the Chalukyas set fire to the fields around. Pulakesin II made another invasion, but he had to pay for it dearly. He was forced to retreat to his capital Vatapi. This time the Pallavas turned the tables back on the Chalukyas. Vatapi was besieged and Pulakesin II was killed by Narasimhavarman I (630–668), son of Mahendravarman I (600–630), at the Battle of Vatapi.

When the Cholas decimated the Pallavas and appropriated the city later in the ninth century, it continued to survive as a *managaram*, thanks to its status as a manufacturing and export centre. In the 11th century, the city had a huge population of about 48,000 and it can be gauged from the fact that 'the large number of streets would indicate how populous the city was and how the weavers, oil-mongers, cloth merchants and the *Nanadesis* with trans-regional trade affiliations had thronged in the city'. Two classes of silk weavers, the *Pattusali*, had set up shop in the four quarters of the city. They had close connections with the temple, managing its accounts, and perhaps using the endowment money as capital for their manufactures, or at the minimum helping themselves to preferential loans from the temple corpus. The merchants were the wealth managers of temple funds, not just in Kanchipuram but also in other cities, and the bigger the temple corpus, the bigger the operations of the merchants.

Vatapi (Badami)

The city of Vatapi, the regal capital of the Badami Chalukyas from 540 to 757 CE, takes its name from the Sanskrit root meaning 'having the wind as an ally'. The city is still standing today in Bagalkot district of Karnataka. It is known for its famous rock-cut monuments as well as structural temples. It stands near a ravine and Agastya Lake. A rugged, sandstone outcrop towers over the city and the lake.

When Pulakesin I founded the Badami Chalukya dynasty in 540 CE, he decided to have Vatapi as his capital. The decision was well-founded since the city was protected by the sandstone cliffs on three sides.

Figure 26: *Vatapi and the sages*

Journey of the city

> **THE ASURA CALLED VATAPI**
>
> The name of the city is also linked to the mythical asura, Vatapi. The story, related in the Mahabharata, is about two demon brothers, Vatapi and Ilvala. Vatapi was a shape changer. He would change into a goat, be cooked by Ilavala, and then offered to visiting sages. Once the sages ate the cooked meat, Vatapi would recompose himself and tear out of the sages' stomachs, killing the victims. The sage Agastya, aware of the asuras' trick, decided to teach them a lesson. He ate the cooked goat offered by Ilvala. But using his enormous powers of ingestion, the sage digested the goat, making it impossible for Vatapi to recompose himself.

Inscriptions reveal that the hill fortress of the city was planned and constructed by the king in 543 CE. It was strategically located on the sandstone cliff. The building of the fortress in the hilly region testifies to the advanced technical skills of builders of those times.

His sons Kirtivarman I and Mangalesa made the city famous by constructing the cave temples that still exist today. Somewhere in the seventh century, Agastya Lake was constructed presumably to serve as a water source for the city. And many temples were also constructed near the city.

After the brothers, the dynasty passed into the hands of Pulakesin II, the son of Kirtivarman in 610 CE. At the height of the dynasty, Vatapi was the capital of a large area that included much of modern Karnataka, Maharashtra, parts of Tamil Nadu, and Andhra Pradesh.

Though the fortress was considered impenetrable, it was destroyed by the Pallava King Narasimhavarman in 643 CE in retaliation for the siege of his capital Kanchipuram by the Chalukyan king. Located very near the city are two other well-known cultural and

Figure 27: *A group of Bhuthanatha Temples on the eastern end of the Agastya Tirtha lake at Badami*

commercial centres, Pattadakkal, possessing a significant number of temples, and Aihole, a commercial centre of repute and the headquarters of the Aihole mercantile guild.

Just before the attack on the city by the Pallava King, the Chinese monk Xuanzang had visited the city.

The *mandapa* style

The Chalukyans built many temples in the *mandapa* style, where the temple has a pillared hall, or *mandapa,* in front and a shrine at the rear or sides. They were adept at working with the soft sandstone available in the area to create large temple structures.

At Badami, there are four structures of the *mandapa* type, of which, two are dedicated to Vishnu, one each to Shiva and the Jaina tirthankaras. The earliest of them was built by Mangalesa. The pillars of the structures are massive, with a square section fitted with corbels supporting a beam.

The Rashtrakutas and the later Chalukyas continued to develop temple architecture and sculpture at Badami. The Northern Bhutanatha group of temples and the Yellamma Temple, completed in the thirteenth century are striking examples.

MANDAPA STYLE OF TEMPLE ARCHITECTURE

In a Hindu temple, a *mandapa* is a pillared hall for public rituals. It is a porch-like structure that leads into the temple and is used for religious dancing and music.

There was always a contest of ownership of Badami and the nearby areas amongst the kings of the Vijayanagara Empire and the Sultans of the Deccan region. To fend off these attacks, the Vijayanagara kings strengthened the fort walls in Badami. Even today, the Fort and some surviving temples stand testimony to the rich heritage of the city.

During the rule of the Sultanates that followed the Vijayanagara period, more structures of heritage value were added. Proof of this are the two monuments, the Markaj Jumma near the entrance of the cave and structural temples and the second – the dargah of Sayyid Hazrat Badshah–near the Upper Shivalaya.

Takeaways

- For a period of three centuries from the sixth to the ninth centuries, the Deccan and South India were dominated by the Chalukyas of Badami, the Pallavas of Kanchipuram, and the Pandyas of Madurai.
- The Chalukyas, weakened by the eighth century, had their place filled up by others.
- Kanchipuram, the Pallava capital, was a manufacturing, trading, and religious centre, constantly suffering as a result of the wars between the Pallavas and the Chalukyas.
- Vatapi, the capital of the Chalukyas, is known for its famous rock-cut monuments.

Fact-check (answers at the back)

1. From the sixth to ninth centuries, Deccan and the South were dominated by the Chalukyas, Pallavas, and the Pandyas. (Yes/No)

2. Kanchipuram was the capital of the Pandya Kingdom. (Yes/No)

3. Vatapi was destroyed by the Pallava King Narasimhavarman. (Yes/No)

4. Madurai was the capital of:
   a. Chalukyas
   b. Yadavas
   c. Cholas
   d. Pandyas

5. Pulakesin II was a Chalukyan king. (Yes/No)

CITIES OF THE CHOLA EMPIRE

(848–1279 CE)

AS WE REACH THE PERIOD OF THE CHOLA EMPIRE, WE NOTICE THAT THE CITIES STARTED PLAYING MULTIPLE ROLES: THEY WERE 'POLITICAL CENTRES, CENTRES OF MANUFACTURING AND TRADE, AND AS SACRED OR CEREMONIAL CENTRES'.

The Kaveri delta had always been the most important resource base for kingdoms from ancient times, but particularly from the seventh century onwards, about three centuries before Rajaraja Chola, the control of this region determined the dominant power in the South. The delta attracted conquerors from the north and south offering them wealth and power.

> **TEMPLES OF CHOLA DYNASTY**
>
> The Chola period is noted for construction of temples that were the nuclei of settlement. They were the hub of economic, religious, social, and cultural life.
>
> The Brihadeeswara temple at Thanjavur, the Brihadeeswara temple at Gangaikondacholapuram, and the Airavateswara temple at Darasuram are some of the most famous temples built during Chola period.

At its zenith, in the eleventh century, the Chola Empire would grow into one of the half-dozen greatest powers on earth and control about half a million square miles–more than five times the size of Britain. One factor for this stupendous achievement was the rise of the cities and the growth of productive forces.

The temple in the cities played the role of employer, landowner, consumer of goods, and services and, more importantly, of a banker. But not all economic activity emanated from or around the temple. The cities were extensively linked with the hinterland, markets, ports, and overseas trade posts through a maze of trade networks. The urban economy and trade were controlled by the corporate assemblies of merchants in the cities, the *nagarams*, with its members called the *nagarattar*. 'The *nagaram* was the link in a hierarchy of markets, linking the villages to the market town, which was linked to higher order centres like the *managarams* (big cities) and port towns.' It collected taxes and functioned as the city government.

The cities and their economic composition

The poets and inscriptions claim that the *nagarams* pulsed with economic activity. The *nagaram* had the 'kadai; the shops, angadi; the markets or bazaars, and the perangadi; the big market in the inner city, the wholesale market'. Streets and main roads crisscrossed in the city. The *nagaram* had its social hierarchy as much as the rest of the Chola society. Its membership was broad-based, consisting of merchants, Vellala landowners, Sankarapadi oil merchants, Saliyar weavers, and fishermen, and the lower order artisans like carpenters, masons, goldsmiths, and leather workers. But the control of the corporate body rested with the top layer who had capital to invest and royal patronage to hang on. The existence of *nagarams* for different occupations increased specialization in marketing. Craftsmen used advanced techniques for production. The earlier cumbersome hand oil mills were promptly replaced with bullock-driven oil mills, improving production manifold. The textile weaving industry was given a facelift and textile looms mushroomed.

The city quarters were called the *kammanacheri,* where goldsmiths, coppersmiths, blacksmiths, carpenters, and sculptors lived, must have been a busy area. The members of the Vishwakarma *kula*, the *Kammalars*, as these craftsmen were called as a professional group, also had their own *jati* affiliations. The *Kammalars* were craftsmen, on a higher social plane than the artisans. They had better opportunities than their rural counterparts who led a stagnant life. The urban artisans benefited from the expanding market and the temple economy. They were mobile and could band together into associations fetching them more bargaining power. However, withdrawal of patronage to temples and the fall of dynasties affected their fortunes.

The ballooning demand for buildings, stone engravings, sculptures, and frescos, not to mention coins and jewellery, provided ample opportunities for craftsmen to move up the caste ladder. One could almost draw a straight line from the professional elevation of craftsmen to their breaking of the Shudra shackle.

Kudandai (Kumbakonam)

Figure 28: *Patteeswaram temple tower near Kumbakonam*

The capture of Kudandai (present-day Kumbakonam) and Thanjavur was crucial for establishing the Chola Empire for they were the growth engines of the southern economy.

Under the imperial Cholas, the Kudandai complex covered a larger area than the present-day city and it had twin cities, Kudamukku and Pazhayarai. It contained four *nadus*; agrarian administrative units, within it.

Major economic activity was centred round the Nageshwara temple, that the royal family reconstructed from its modest existence. The temple records 'endowments made in the form of land, cows, sheep, gold, and money'. Apart from the royal family, these endowments were made from Chola officials of high rank, local merchants, traders from distant lands like Kerala, and large *Vellala* landowners from various parts of the empire. Closely associated with the temple were Brahmanas, shepherds, members of the *Kaikkolar* weaver community, and others. The temple coffers were filled with staggering amounts of gold lumps and Chola gold coins–the *kazhanju*. There is a record of an assembly in the city raising gold through sale of land to meet the hefty demand of Paranataka I of 3,000 *kazhanju* of gold (roughly 15.6 kg) to fund his Pandya wars.

The city was an important hub on the trade grid of the South, 'a centre of betel nut and areca nut cultivation' as well as a preferred source for metal work and textiles. There was even a Chola mint in the city. The twin cities 'were knitted to their rural and coastal hinterlands through intricate ties'.

Pazhayarai

Pazhayarai, the twin city of Kumbakonam, served more as a residential stronghold for the imperial Cholas. The Chola kings not only built residential palaces but also contributed to erecting temples, for which they contributed generously.

> **TEMPLE TOWN**
>
> Kumbakonam is popularly known as a temple town and is home to about 188 temples.
>
> The town is noted for its Mahamaham festival, which happens once every twelve years, attracting people from all over country.

The city was also a military centre, with army cantonments surrounding the palace area. In spite of the fact that the more successful Cholas like Rajaraja Chola 'chose Thanjavur for their monumental edifices and rich benefactions', the city never ceased to function as an administrative centre. Rajaraja's father Sundara Chola called himself the king of Nandipuram, the other name for Pazhaiyarai. The importance of Pazhayarai and the adjoining region can be seen from the fact that Rajaraja brought a large number of employees from these areas to take care of the Thanjavur temple, the iconic centre of the Chola Empire. Among the employees were four hundred temple women and a host of support staff such as musicians, barbers, carpenters, and goldsmiths.

The incentive to move into the capital city would have been irresistible since each employee was granted a piece of land to build their houses.

Thanjavur

Thanjavur, the new administrative capital of the Cholas, was located in the south-western edge of the rich Kaveri delta region on the southern bank of the Vadavaru River.

The city was occupied, and a settlement had existed there in pre-Chola times. But a phenomenal transformation during the Chola times catapulted the city into a major royal and temple city. And it became the most powerful and prestigious city south of the Godavari in those times.

Thanjavur had a central location in the Kaveri basin and on the trade network. Considering this, the Cholas were willing to sacrifice the legitimacy they would have acquired easily had they continued to keep the ancient and historic city of Uraiyur, the centre of the Sangam era Cholas, as their capital.

The city of Thanjavur expanded around the imposing Brihadeeswara temple at its core, with its tall *vimana* and *gopurams* forming the city's skyline. The area around the temple formed the downtown with multi-storeyed mansions housing the city's political and priestly elites. The outer circle housed the next most powerful class, the rich merchants. The city boasted of four *angadis*, the markets, catering a variety of goods to different strata with different opening and closing hours. The temple generated considerable demand for milk, ghee, and flowers, as well as services of 'priests, temple women, musicians, washermen, and watchmen'.

The iconic Brihadeeswara Temple

The Brihadeeswara temple, situated at the centre of the city, was a cultural and artistic emporium. Special performances and festivals commemorating royal birthdays and festivals (never in short supply) kept the temple grounds crowded and busy throughout the year. Donations poured in not only from the royal family but from high-ranking officers, wealthy merchants, and big landlords. Regular contributions came in from surrounding villages and colonised territories, not to speak of sudden spurts of income from the spoils and loot from war. Revenue accruing

Figure 29: *Brihadeeswara Temple in Thanjavur*

from as many as forty villages in Cholamandalam, the core area of the state, and another sixteen villages in conquered territories, such as Karnataka and Lanka, flowed into the temple's coffers. The temple was a massive corporate entity even by today's standards, employing around six hundred people. Elaborate arrangements were made by the king for the provision and maintenance of services with 'sixty-seven lamps being lit every day, of at least one hundred and forty-five watchmen being on the payroll, about three hundred and sixty-nine places giving or receiving resources to it'. But it is to be noted that despite all of the above information, the city drew its fibre not just from the temple but also from its myriad connections with manufacturing and trade networks.

The city with seven-fold walls

The Chinese documenter Zhao Rukuo described the city even more grandiosely. According to his effusive description, the city had seven-fold walls each seven feet high and the city itself measured 6.6 km long and 3.9 km wide, quite large for those times. Each wall was about one hundred, and the innermost of wood. The outer walls were surrounded by streams and the main people's quarters were within the first three walls from the outer edge. Ministers occupied the space inside the fourth wall and princes, the fifth. The sixth wall enclosed Buddhist monasteries and the seventh wall comprised the royal palace with a huge array of four hundred rooms. The temple was left out of the description and the presence of one hundred Buddhist monks near the centre sounds fanciful but probable.

> **THANJAVUR AND THE CHOLA EMPIRE**
>
> Thanjavur attained prominence under the mighty Cholas and emerged as the cradle of Tamil civilizations. The Cholas were not just rulers, they were great builders as well. And that can be witnessed in the large number of exquisite temples in the city.

The city was a microcosm of the empire's best and worst. Traders and artisans flocked from all corners of the empire and from beyond. People speaking several tongues walked its streets and bylanes. The city sucked up the empire's resources and talents like a sponge – its money, artisans, craftsmen, traders, and musicians. Conventional religious sects battled with the heterodox ones for recognition and patronage. It started with multi-storeyed mansions at the centre and ended up with despicable hovels at the periphery. It was a place of appalling contrasts. Yet to say this would mean overlooking the finest collection of stone and brass sculptures, the stunningly colourful festivals, the grandness of the emperor's palaces, the fine rhythm of the grand temple's othuvars when they recited the hymns, and the dance and drama extravaganzas which might have put Indra's pageants to shame.

OTHUVARS ARE TRADITIONAL SINGERS WHO CHANT THE SAIVITE TAMIL DEVOTIONAL HYMNS IN TEMPLES DURING THE MAIN PUJA PERIOD.

Tirunelveli

The ancient city of Tirunelveli is believed to be at least 2000 years old. But excavations in Adichanallur, just 15 kms away, point to the existence of a civilization almost as old as the Harappan civilization. Clay urns and human skeletons unearthed in the site in 2005 were found to be atleast 3800 years old. Carbon dating of another set of samples revealed that they belonged to a society which existed around 1000 BCE.

Another site discovered about 15 kms further away from Adichannalur and within 40 kms of Tirunelveli is Korkai, an ancient port of the Pandyan Kingdom of the Sangam period. At that time, about 2500 years ago, it was located at the junction of the Tamiraparani River and the Bay of Bengal which formed a natural harbour. At that time its fame as a pearl fishery spread far and wide. The ancient Greek traveller Ptolemy refers to the port as an Emporium. The *Periplus* also confirms the existence of this port. Since then the sea has receded and Korkai town lies about 6 km inland. It is no longer a port or a city of importance.

In the same manner as Adichanallur, the existence of megalithic burial urns in Korkai confirms the existence of a well settled population in those ancient times. Carbon dating of these artefacts tell us that they are 2800 years old. The pottery found in these sites.

The surprising fact is that all the three sites lying within a 15 km radius were unearthed in the early or mid-nineteenth century but only 150 years later serious excavations have thrown up phenomenal results.

A timeline of **Tirunelveli**

- At least **3800** years old. — Burial urns found near the city
- Age of the city — At least two millennia
- **1877** BCE — Bishop Robert Caldwell's research on the town
- Pandyas of the Sangam period — **Fourth century** BCE **to Third century** CE
- **Fourth to fifth centuries** CE — Early Pallavas
- Rajendra Chola I conquers Tirunelveli — **1064** CE
- **1306** CE — Captured by Vijayanagara Empire
- Comes under the rule of Madurai Nayaks — **1529** CE

Korkai was identified by archaeological excavations in 1838. But only recently carbon dating of artefacts were done revealing that they belong to a period around 785 BCE. Red and black pottery with Tamil-Brahmi scripts inscribed on them have been discovered. In addition, graffiti in the shape of the sun, fish and arrow appear to have been created between the third century BCE and the second century CE. Roman ware and rouletted ware are proof of trade with western countries.

Adichanallur was first discovered in 1876 by a scientist from Berlin called F. Jagor. He was assisted by the then acting Collector of Tirunelveli and the District Engineer of the British colonial regime. They found earthen utensils, iron implements and skeletal remains in burial sites. While he informed the government, Dr Jagor took away the artefacts to the Berlin Museum depriving future researchers of valuable evidence. About twenty years later, Dr Alexander Rea of the ASI wanted to investigate further and did large excavation followed by others. Dr Rea reported his findings in many publications.

Dr Rea unearthed more than a thousand objects and among them were iron implements and weapons, bronze and gold ornaments, household stone implements such as grinders, traces of cloth and mica, rice and millet.

In 2004, more surprises emerged. Burial urns were found containing skeletons of the dead not only of Tamil origin but also that of Australoid, Southeast Asian and East Asian origin!

Carbon dating of the samples established that period of the archaeological findings must have spanned from 905 BCE to 696 BCE.

Such recent archaeological findings have had a major impact on the understanding that historians had about the Tamil civilization. The towns in this region could have been cosmopolitan like Chennai since different ethnic groups lived in them. The earlier understanding was that there was a single ethnic group living in these areas who can be termed as the original Dravidians. These settlements, spread over a radius of 15 km, could have been big settlements, well-connected by river and sea routes, and engaged in trade with the outside world. There is also the hypothesis that the script of the Harappan Civilizations is linked to the Tamil-Brahmi script engraved on artefacts in areas such as Adichanallur, Keeladi and Arikamedu. This implies that when the Harappan Civilization declined, they may have moved south.

Now coming back to Tirunelveli, Bishop Robert Caldwell, who was the Bishop of Tirunelveli during the year 1877 as well as a competent linguist, did an extensive research on the town. He studied the Sangam literature and also poured through palm leaf manuscripts to get a grip on the history of the city. He also conducted excavations discovering coins and funeral urns.

Caldwell's study confirmed that Tirunelveli city is at least two millennia old and the age of the settlements in the vicinity of the city are even older. Like many other cities of the Tamil region, Tirunelveli changed hands several times. During the Sangam Age, the Pandya chieftains ruled over the city. Tirunelveli was the secondary capital of the Pandyas, Madurai being the primary. After that it fell into the hands of the Cheras.

When the Chola Empire peaked in the tenth and eleventh centuries, the city was ruled by the medieval Cholas and the Later Cholas. Rajendra Chola I brought the city under his control in 1064. The city remained under the Cholas till the thirteenth century.

After the decline of the Cholas, the city fell into the hands of the

THERE IS ALSO THE HYPOTHESIS THAT THE SCRIPT OF THE HARAPPAN CIVILIZATIONS IS LINKED TO THE TAMIL-BRAHMI SCRIPT

Figure 30: Nellaiyappar Temple in Tirunelveli

Pandyas again. The Nelliappar Temple, a monument which served as the royal shrine of the Pandyas, exists even today. With the end of the Pandyan dynasty with the death of Kulasekara Pandian (1268–1308), the city was captured by the Vijayanagara Empire who held sway until the region was subdued by the British. The Marava chieftains, called the Palayakkarar, controlled parts of the region. In the sixteenth century, Viswanatha Nayak (1529–64), was appointed as the Viceroy of Madurai for his allegiance to the Vijayanagara Empire. He founded the Madurai Nayak dynasty. Tirunelveli city was rebuilt in his reign.

Takeaways

- During the Chola Empire, many cities developed into political, manufacturing, trade, and religious centres.
- In its heyday in the eleventh century, the Chola Empire was one of the half-dozen greatest powers on earth.
- The cities had their social hierarchy. Traders, craftsmen, and artisans who had migrated to cities enjoyed a certain level of social mobility compared to their rural counterparts.
- The Kudanthai complex (present-day Kumbakonam) served both as an industrial and residential complex for the Cholas.
- During the Chola period, large temples served as corporate entities also generating demand for goods and employing thousands of people.
- The Chinese documenter, Zhao Rukup, has described Thanjavur in his writings.

Fact-check (answers at the back)

1. Cities played multiple roles as political, manufacturing, trade and religious centres. (Yes/No)

2 The nagaram linked villages to the market town. (Yes/No)

3 Craftsmen who migrated to cities had better economic and social opportunities. (Yes/No)

4 The Kudanthai complex was made of the twin cities of Kudamukku and Pazhayarai. (Yes/No)

5 The administrative capital of the Cholas was:
   a. Madurai
   b. Thanjavur
   c. Kumbakonam
   d. Muziris

NEWER CITIES OF THE DECCAN (THIRTEENTH–FOURTEENTH CENTURY)

TOWARDS THE MIDDLE OF THE TWELFTH CENTURY, THE IMPERIAL CHOLAS WANED IN POWER. THIS CREATED THE OPTION FOR NEW KINGDOMS AND POWER EQUATIONS TO RISE. THE PANDYAS REVIVED THEIR POWER AND ATTACKED THE CHOLAS AND ALSO ATTEMPTED TO CAPTURE LANKA AND KERALA.

The Hoysalas, who had freed themselves from the Chalukyas, sided with the Cholas to stop the Pandyas from advancing.

From the north, the Kakatiyas, with their capital in Warangal, also waged war on the Cholas. The Kakatiya Kingdom reached its height of power under Ganapati (1199–1262). And finally, the rule of the Cholas ended in 1279.

Meanwhile, the Yadavas freed themselves from the Chalukyas and established their capital at Devagiri.

New cities flourished under these new kingdoms. However, at the beginning of the fourteenth century, the Hoysalas, Kakatiyas, Pandyas, and Yadavas came under attack by the Delhi Sultanate. In 1310, Warangal was pillaged by the Malik Kafur, the general of the Khalji ruler of the second Delhi Sultanate. Though all the four powers in the South were overcome by Malik Kafur, these

Figure 31: Ancient Daulatabad fort near Aurangabad

territories were just raided and not conquered. But a little later, Muhammad bin Tughluq occupied all these territories.

The Tughluqs created their power centres in several cities of the Deccan and the South such as Devagiri, Gulbarga, Warangal, and Madurai.

While there was a major shift in power centres, a power arose in the city of Hampi around 1340, emerging into the new state of Vijayanagara, which brought the massive area south of the Tungabhadra and Krishna under its umbrella.

Almost simultaneously, to the north of these rivers, a new Sultanate called the Bahmani Kingdom was established in 1347.

So, for about two hundred years, stretching over the thirteenth and fourteenth centuries, South India was ravaged by wars and anarchy. This re-established the fact that when the Indian subcontinent was riven by internecine wars and lack of unity among rulers, it becomes vulnerable to external occupation.

Let us look at a few of the cities which served as power centres during this period.

Hampi

The city of Hampi was the capital of the Vijayanagara Empire in the fourteenth century. It was a well-fortified city. Persian and European travellers have attested to the fact that the city near the Tungabhadra was prosperous and impressive. It was a religious as well as a trading centre.

By 1500 CE, at its peak, the city was the world's second-largest medieval-era city after Beijing, and probably India's richest at that time, attracting traders from Persia and Portugal. It was the capital of an empire which covered about 140,000 square miles .

The city was reduced to rubble when the Vijayanagara Empire was defeated by a coalition of the Deccan Sultanates in 1565.

Hampi's ruins are spread over 16 square miles, near the modern city of Hosapete. According to UNESCO, it is an 'austere, grandiose site' of more than 1,600 surviving remains of the Vijayanagara empire that includes 'forts, riverside features, royal and sacred complexes, temples, shrines, pillared halls, mandapas, memorial structures, water structures and others'. These surviving artefacts attest to the sophistication of architecture and art in those times.

BY 1500 CE, AT ITS PEAK, HAMPI WAS THE WORLD'S SECOND-LARGEST MEDIEVAL-ERA CITY AFTER BEIJING, AND PROBABLY INDIA'S RICHEST AT THAT TIME, ATTRACTING TRADERS FROM PERSIA AND PORTUGAL. IT WAS THE CAPITAL OF AN EMPIRE WHICH COVERED ABOUT 140,000 SQUARE MILES

Temples as the centre of townships

Several temple complexes have been unearthed in the region. They confirm that Dravidian temple complexes were at the centre

Figure 32: *Virupaksha Temple in Hampi on the banks of Tungabhadra River*

of suburban townships called *puras*, containing bazaars and residential areas. The city had tanks employing unique hydrological technologies. The remains unearthed at the site point towards the existence of a highly developed society possessing economic prosperity and an evolved political system.

The temples in the city display the continuation of the Dravidian architecture adopted by the Pallavas, Pandyas, and Cholas. The temples are endowed with lofty *mandapas* and *gopurams,* cloistered enclosures for the deity, and pillared halls.

The Vitthala temple is the apogee of temple architecture of the period. It has three *gopurams* and several *manadapams*. Besides these, it has a Garuda shrine in the shape of a granite *ratha* and a grand bazaar street. The temple complex also has a large *Pushkarani* (stepped tank) and a *Vasantotsava mandapa* (ceremonial pavilion at the centre), wells, and a network of water channels. The roofs were laid with the heavy thick granite slabs covered with a water-proof course of brick jelly and lime mortar.

A unique feature of the temple complexes is that they had wide streets for taking out chariots during festivals. The streets are flanked by pillared *mandapas*.

Most of the structures at Hampi were built with local granite, burnt bricks, and lime mortar. The city also had massive fortification walls built with irregular cut-size stones. The joints were filled with rubble masonry without any binding material.

Vijayanagara architecture incorporated Indo-Islamic elements in secular buildings, like the Queen's Bath and the Elephant Stables, representing a highly evolved multi-religious and multi-ethnic society.

The construction activity in Hampi for over two hundred years reflected the progress in art, architecture, and political and spiritual life that the empire had achieved. Finally, the Battle of Talikota (1565 CE) resulted in its destruction.

Even today, Hampi continues to be an important religious centre, with its Virupaksha Temple, an active Adi Shankara-linked monastery, and various monuments belonging to the old city.

BATTLE OF TALIKOTA

The Battle of Talikota was a historic battle fought between the forces of the Vijayanagara Empire and the allied forces of the Sultanates of Bijapur, Bidar, Ahmadnagar, and Golconda.

The battle took place in 1565 near Bijapur, in northern Karnataka. The armies collectively numbered at several hundred thousand, and there were large contingents of elephants. The capital city Hampi was destroyed in the battle. The superior artillery power of the Sultanates decided the outcome of the battle in their favour.

Warangal

Before being elevated to the status of the capital of the

A timeline of Warangal Fort

1199–1262 Ganapathideva replaces brick wall of Fort with a stone wall.

1262–1289 Rudrammadevi, his daughter, completed the stone wall and also built an outer wall.

1295–1326 Fort further strengthened by her grandson Prataparudra II

1309 Malik Kafur, the general of Alauddin Khalji, lays siege to the Fort.

1323 The Delhi Sultanate ruler's son Muhammad bin Tughluq captures the Fort.

Kakatiya dynasty, Warangal was under the control of the Rashtrakuta dynasty in the eighth century. Later, it passed into the hands of the Chalukyan Empire in the tenth century. It was during the rule of King Ganapathideva (1199–1262) that the Kaktiya capital was moved from Hanamkonda to Warangal. Inscriptions belonging to that period speak of Warangal as the best city of the Telugu region.

The city stands today as the second largest city of the state of Telengana. Many monuments left by the Kakatiyas including fortresses, lakes, temples, and stone gateways have now helped the city to become a popular tourist attraction.

Ganapathideva started the building of the inner stone wall of Warangal. His daughter, Rudrammadevi (1262–1289), who succeeded him after his death, ruled for thirty years and was in power when Marco Polo, an Italian merchant, explorer and writer visited India. In Marco Polo's words, she was a wise and well-loved queen, who remained a widow for her husband's sake and ruled his kingdom well.

The Kakatiyas were defeated by Delhi Sultanate in 1323, who

Figure 33: The Thousand Pillar Temple or Rudreshwara Swamy Temple, Hanamakonda

renamed the city as Sultanpur. Later the Nayaks recaptured Warangal in 1336. And, after the downfall of the Nayaks, Warangal was annexed by the Bahmani Sultanate followed by the Sultanate of Golconda.

The Temple of a Thousand Pillars

The earliest of the monuments that has survived is the magnificent temple of one thousand pillars at Hanamkonda. This temple was built by Prataparudradeva I, the grandson of Rudrammadevi. It exhibits the best features of Chalukyan architecture and is dedicated to the god Rudra, the main deity of the Kakatiyas. A long Sanskrit inscription carved on a square pillar provides details of the Kakatiyas. Surprisingly, the temple also contains another later inscription, which speaks highly of the heroism of a Muhammadan general named Shitab Khan. The existence of a Sanskrit inscription in a Hindu temple praising a Muhammadan general indicates that the general was held in high esteem.

Only four gates of the large temple at Warangal have survived the ravages of time. Even the enclosing walls have been destroyed. But, from the large area enclosed by the walls and the exquisite carving of the stones removed from the temple and used for the repair of the fort wall, it can be deduced that the Warangal temple was better than the temple of a thousand pillars at Hanamkonda in its aesthetics.

The area enclosed by the earthen wall built by Rudrammadevi, which is about two miles, was occupied by the city of Warangal. Within the boundaries of the inner stone wall lay the temples, palaces of the raja, and the elite. There is a third outer wall, also of earth, whose remains are distinctly visible and which enclosed an area of about 12.5 km in diameter. The use of this outer rampart is not clear because the city could not have stretched to such a large area encompassed by the rampart. A possible explanation could be that the rampart enclosed the suburbs of the city too.

A timeline of **Devagiri**

1187 The city was in prominence as an important town from the sixth century. But the first Yadava king, Bhillama V, built a fortress and made the city his capital in the 12th century.

1294 The city was annexed and plundered by Alauddin Khilji of the Khilji dynasty.

1327 After the Tughluq dynasty overtook the Khilji dynasty, Muhammad bin Tughluq named the city Daulatabad and moved his capital here.

1334 Muhammad bin Tughluq reversed his decision, and Delhi again was made the capital of the Delhi Sultanate.

1499 Daulatabad became a part of Ahmadnagar Sultanate and most of the fortifications at the fort was done at this time.

Devagiri

The city of Devagiri has an outstanding fort and citadel and served as a capital of an empire; therefore, it is a mystery why the city has remained relatively obscure till today.

The city, renamed

Daulatabad by Muhammad bin Tughluq in the fourteenth century, has an imposing, fortified citadel and is located near Aurangabad, Maharashtra. It served as the capital of the Yadava dynasty from the ninth to fourteenth century. Thereafter, it was briefly the capital of the Delhi Sultanate and later a secondary capital of the Ahmadnagar Sultanate.

The 600-feet high rock mass forming the citadel can be seen from miles around. But for reasons unknown, it has not received the attention it deserves from archaeologists and visitors. The town rests on a conical hill of rock rising abruptly from the surrounding

Figure 34: *Ruins at Devagiri Fort in Daulatabad*

plains. It probably dates at least from the first century BCE and lies on the highway connecting Ellora and other ancient cities. The natural citadel sitting on a highway would have been the obvious choice for dynasties and empires as a fortress. But it remained a site with rock-cut caves until it appears in the historical records in the twelfth century CE in the name of Devagiri. As a hill so strongly fortified by nature, the citadel town would have required a minimum of artificial defences. The rock-cut caves are accessible today through a system of underground passages carved out when the fort was constructed.

Figure 35: Panorama of Devagiri Fort in Daulatabad

Devagiri grows in importance

From the sixth century, Devagiri emerged as an important town lying on caravan routes going west and south. But it was in 1187, that the Yadava King Billamma extended his territory southwards to the Krishna River and founded his capital here. So it is to him that this magnificent piece of fortification should be attributed to. The superb technique employed confirmed the fact that the quarrymen who constructed the Kailasa temple at Ellora had successfully

> **WILD POLICY SWINGS**
>
> Daulatabad was situated at a central place and administrating the north and south could be easier from here. It is said that the general public of Delhi was not in favour of shifting base. However, because of the grants given to all immigrants and administrative work being done from the 'second capital', people moved to Daulatabad.
>
> But, a few years and a few revolts later, Mohammad bin Tughlaq feared that the northern borders were exposed to attacks and he shifted his capital back to Delhi.
>
> As an administrative measure, this decision failed but the spread of Urdu in the Deccan could be attributed to this decision.

DELHI TO DAULATABAD

Muhammad Ibn Battuta was a Moroccan traveller who left his home at a young age of twenty-one in the thirteenth century to travel across the world. During his thirty years of travelling, he visited around forty-four countries, including India. He published his travelling accounts in the book the *Rihlah*, which means 'travels', a part of which is devoted to his experience in India.

He entered India in 1333 and reached the royal court of Mohammad bin Tughlaq, the then ruler of Delhi. Mohammed bin Tughlaq was impressed, and Battuta was given a furnished house and a job of Qadi (Judge) in the royal court. The traveller historian stayed for around seven years.

He witnessed the forced migration of Delhi's population to Daulatabad. And described the picture of the sultan standing on the roof of his palace at night and looking out over Delhi 'where there was neither fire nor smoke nor lamp' and saying 'now my mind is tranquil and my wrath appeased'. He also wrote about Dellhi in his memoirs, 'It was almost a desert, the greatest city in the world had the fewest inhabitants.'

Figure 36: Daulatabad, fourteenth-century fort city, 16 km northwest of Aurangabad

handed over their skills to their successors. The scarping of the sides of the hill to a vertical rock-cut face of 150 to 200 feet high and the presence of a water-filled moat at the bottom, dug 50 feet into solid rock, is astonishing. The town also extended to suburbs below the citadel resting over the gently sloping ground to the east.

While by the end of the twelfth century, the Sultanate of Delhi had been established on the northwest Indian plains, the Deccan was free of incursions. This changed in 1294, when Alauddin Khalji, the nephew of Jalauddin, and the founder of the Khalji dynasty, raided the Deccan and attacked Devagiri during the rule of Yadava King Ramachandra.

The forces of Alauddin plundered the lower city while the Raja retreated to the citadel. When Ramachandra's son engaged the invading forces in a battle outside the city, he suffered a disastrous loss. And Alauddin returned with the plunder made at Devagiri. With this success under his belt, he murdered his uncle, seized the throne, and made Devagiri a vassal.

After the Khalji dynasty was overtaken by the Tughlaq dynasty, Devagiri was renamed Daulatabad by Mohammed bin Tughlaq (1325–51) in 1327. It was during this period that the Sultan took the stupefying decision to move not only the seat of his government but the residents as well from Delhi to Daulatabad, over a distance of 700 miles, much to the chagrin of the entire population of Delhi. So Daulatabad was suddenly elevated to the grand position of the capital of the powerful Tughlaq dynasty, only to be restored to its previous state in 1334, when the Sultan realised his folly and shifted the capital back to Delhi.

The Ashlar masonry that can be witnessed in the fort was done during this period.

In the mid-seventeenth century, the outer town of Daulatabad was known as Amberkot. The sultan built a second line of defence around the main fort called the Mahakot, the great fort.

In the outer portion of the Mahakot stands the Chand Minar, built in 1445 under the Bahmani dynasty, who took over the city from the Tughlaqs. This area consists of mosques and a ruined group of palaces. It also has a 'China Palace' used as a state prison after the fall of Golconda and Bijapur in the seventeenth century.

In 1499, Daulatabad was annexed by the Ahmadnagar Sultanate, who used it as their secondary capital. Most of the present-day fortifications at Daulatabad Fort were constructed under the Ahmadnagar Sultanate.

About the Fort, Ibn Battuta wrote that the fort was accessed by a leather ladder in the night. He was perhaps not fully aware of the maze of underground passages built for accessing the fort. The fort has a set of winding passages, guard chambers, and modified rock caves, forming an ingenious complex of subterranean approaches to the fort, which are marvelled at even today. There are secret chambers which must have been guarded by swordsmen. At the end of the final stairway into the fort, a sliding iron trapdoor was fabricated, which could be made red hot by a huge fire in case of enemy incursion.

Special features of the fort

- A single entrance/exit gate in order to confuse the enemy.
- No parallel gates in order to break the momentum of the invading army.
- Spikes on the gates to keep away elephants from being used as battering rams.
- Complex arrangement of entryways, curved walls, and false doors designed to confuse the enemy.
- Smooth hill side to prevent the use of mountain lizards as climbers.

Takeaways

- After the Imperial Cholas waned in power, several dynasties rose or revived to fill in the void, such as the Pandyas, Hoyaslas, Chalukyas, Kakatiyas and Yadavas.
- New cities flourished under these kingdoms.
- Hampi, Warangal, and Devagiri served as the capitals of the Vijayanagara Empire, Kakatiya dynasty, and the Yadava dynasty respectively.
- At the beginning of the fourteenth century, the Hoysalas, Kakatiyas, Pandyas, and Yadavas came under attack by the Delhi Sultanate.
- A little later, Muhammad bin Tughluq occupied all these territories. The Tughluqs created their power centres in several cities of the Deccan and the South, such as Devagiri, Gulbarga, Warangal, and Madurai.
- In 1340, the Vijayanagara Empire arose with its capital at Hampi.
- Almost simultaneously, to the north of these rivers, a new Sultanate called the Bahmani Kingdom was established in 1347.
- For about two hundred years, stretching over the thirteenth and fourteenth centuries, South India was riven by wars and anarchy.

Fact-check (answers at the back)

1. The rule of the Imperial Cholas came to an end in the thirteenth century. (Yes/No)

2. There was a lot of unity between the new powers of the region. (Yes/No)

3. The Delhi Sultanate not only pillaged the cities in the region but also established their power centres. (Yes/No)

4. Mohammed bin Tughlaq shifted his capital from Delhi to Daulatabad. (Yes/No)

5. The well-known traveller Ibn Battuta visited Daulatabad in 1340. (Yes/No)

6. The city of Devagiri was renamed Daulatabad. (Yes/No)

7. Devagiri is a citadel town, protected by an impregnable fort. (Yes/No)

8. Warangal served as the capital of the:
   a. Cholas
   b. Pandyas
   c. Kakatiyas
   d. Shungas

9. Hampi was the capital of the:
   a. Mauryan Empire
   b. Chola Empire
   c. Pallava Empire
   d. Vijayanagara Empire

CITIES OF THE MUGHAL EMPIRE (1526–1857)

IT WAS A GOLDEN PERIOD FOR URBANIZATION UNDER THE MUGHAL EMPIRE. SOME ESTIMATES REVEAL THAT WITH FIFTEEN PER CENT OF THE POPULATION LIVING IN CITIES, THE LEVEL OF URBANIZATION IN THE MUGHAL EMPIRE WAS EVEN HIGHER THAN THAT IN CONTEMPORARY EUROPE. ONLY IN THE NINETEENTH CENTURY DID EUROPE REACH THIS LEVEL OF URBANIZATION.

Other estimates infer that in the early seventeenth century, during the reign of Akbar, the urban population was an impressive seventeen million. This might have exceeded the entire urban population of Europe at that time. By the early eighteenth century this population expanded to more than twenty-two million. But some scholars have also expressed the opinion that these estimates are far-fetched and that urbanization was much lower at around nine per cent.

According to some sources, there were more than a hundred cities during Akbar's reign with a population ranging from a quarter to a half million. Cities such as Agra, Lahore, Dhaka, and Delhi had a population even higher than these figures.

These numbers have not been validated thoroughly. Nevertheless, it is clear that urbanization reached never-before heights during the Mughal period.

Cities such as Agra, Lahore, Fatehpur Sikri, and Delhi served as Mughal capitals at one point or another. This is not to leave out Kabul, which served as the summer capital for some time. Sometimes the Empire had multiple capitals too, necessitated by the political and military situation or even due to ideological compulsions. Some cities served as provincial capitals. During wars when the king and his entire military entourage was on the move, the administrative capital literally shifted to military camps.

Other than cities serving as capitals, they also served as manufacturing, trading, and religious centres. In the narrative that follows we will be getting acquainted with some of the capital cities of the Mughal Empire.

Agra

Agra has a history of many centuries before Mughal rule but not as a city of importance. The ancient city of Agra gained some prominence when Sikandar Lodhi of the Delhi Sultanate undertook some rebuilding on the left bank of the Yamuna in 1504–1505 CE. At this time the city grew into an important centre of Islamic learning. After Sikander Lodi's death, his son Ibrahim Lodi took over the reins. When he was killed by the Mughal Emperor Babur in the First Battle of Panipat, the city passed into the hands of the Mughals.

But the modern city of Agra, which lies on the right bank of the river, owes its existence to Akbar (1556–1605) who founded it in 1558 CE. It was under his rule that the city flowered into a city acknowledged for its political, cultural, and economic pre-eminence throughout the world. The imposing Agra Fort was built by the emperor. Later, Akbar shifted his capital to Fatehpur Sikri on the basis of ideological and sentimental grounds, but Agra continued to be an urban centre of importance.

The English traveller Ralph Fitch, who visited the cities of Agra and Fatehpur Sikri during Akbar's reign, described the cities as having large streets and busy bazaars. According to him, the cities were even greater than London and had an impressive population.

After Akbar, his successor Jahangir added many embellishments to the monuments in the city. He laid out many gardens. He erected Akbar's mausoleum at Sikandra on the outskirts of Agra. He was also instrumental in the construction of the Jahangiri Mahal in Agra fort and the tomb of Itmad-ud-daulah.

Timeline of **Agra** and the kings of **The Mughal Empire**

- **1504–1505 CE** — Rebuilding of the ancient city Agra by Sikandar Lodi
- **1558 CE** — Founding of the modern city of Agra by Akbar
- **1556–1605 CE** — Akbar
- **1569–1627 CE** — Jahangir
- **1592–1666 CE** — Shah Jahan
- **1618–1707 CE** — Aurangzeb

Jahangir's son, Shah Jahan (1592–1666), in whose hands the Mughal reign passed after his death, made the city popular throughout the world by building the Taj Mahal, considered one of the New Seven Wonders of the World. Like his father he also added many more impressive structures such as the Jama Masjid, the Diwan-i-Am, the Diwan-i-Khas, and the Moti Masjid.

But in the reign of Shah Jahan, Agra began to lose its importance

***Figure 37:** The Taj Mahal*

when the emperor shifted his capital to Shahjahanabad, now popularly known as Old Delhi. It continued to function as the second capital. In terms of its cultural and strategic importance the city retained its original glory.

After the death of Aurangzeb (1618–1707), Shah Jahan's son, the Mughal Empire disintegrated and Agra's importance declined.

Fatehpur Sikri

In the year 1571, Akbar abandoned Agra as the capital and named Fatehpur Sikri as the administrative centre of the empire. This city is only about 35 km from Agra. It continued to be the capital till 1585 CE. The reason for opting for a new capital was both sentimental and ideological. From then on the city's fortunes were dependant on its creators' whims.

The city came up over a village called Sikri and hence the name. The village had been having an active life before Akbar shifted his capital. Archaeological excavations have indicated the existence of houses, temples, and commercial centres. Many centuries back the region had been under the control of the Shunga dynasty (185 to 73 BCE).

Akbar was a great admirer of the Sufi saint Sheikh Salim Chishti, who lived in the area and who had predicted the birth of his first male child. When Jahangir was born in 1569, Akbar decreed that a palace city should be built on the hitherto lonely hilltop of Sikri. First a religious compound was built to commemorate the saint. Then a walled city and the imperial palace came up. It is said that the building of

Figure 38: *Fatehpur Sikri Buland Darwaza*

Figure 39: *A view of the immaculate, abandoned temple complex at Fathepur Sikri*

the palace and other monuments went on for fifteen years during which Akbar visited the city and lived there for short times. In 1573, after a successful Gujarat campaign, when Akbar visited the city, the Sheikh expressed his wish that besides being a ruler Akbar should also become a religious head.

This idea spurred Akbar to build a hall in Fatehpur Sikri called the Ibadat Khana ('House of Worship'). The hall became a regular venue for discussions on matters of spirituality among the best minds in the city. While discussions were restricted to Muslim spirituality initially, Akbar expanded this to include other religions and even atheistic thought.

Fatehpur Sikri lies on an elevated ridge about forty metres high. The city is three km in length and one km in width, surrounded by a wall on three sides stretching six km. The fourth side of the city faces a lake. The neat layout and the proliferation of gardens and monuments were meant to offer comfort and richness to its esteemed residents.

On the south of the city stands the tremendously majestic Buland Darwaza. This was erected as a triumphal gateway in 1575–6 to commemorate the victory of Akbar in the Deccan. It stands 54 metres tall, representing one of the tallest gateways envisaged. From the top of the steps leading to the entrance, one can get a breath-taking view of the plains around. An inscription in the archway cautions the visitor philosophically, 'The world is a bridge, pass over it, but build no houses on it.'

On the west of the high ridge is the magnificent structure, the Jama Masjid, a congregational mosque. It was built five years before the Buland Darwaza. The mosque again has a massive entrance to its courtyard. The mosque combines the finest elements of Indian and Iranian architecture. It was one of the world's largest mosques of that period.

Situated within the courtyard of the grand mosque is the tomb of Sheikh Salim Chisti, the saint who influenced Akbar profoundly. The original building was of sandstone, which was later improved into a white marble building by Jahangir. Intricately pierced stone screens adorn the inside of the tomb. The central shrine is made of ebony and mother-of-pearl.

The Diwan-i-Khas served as a private council chamber for the emperor. It has a unique design. There is a central pillar which supports a circular area on top of its elaborate capital. This is where the emperor used to sit for the council meeting. From the circular area radiated four bridges extending up to the galleries constructed on the walls around. The councillors sat in the galleries at the four ends.

Akbar abandoned his favourite city in 1585, when he had to leave for a campaign in Punjab. After his death, the city became even more neglected. The scarcity of water supply may have been the reason for its abandonment.

A timeline of Lahore

100 CE	Founding of the city.
1021 CE	Captured by Mahmud Ghazni
1163 CE	Becomes capital city of Ghaznavid Empire
1206 CE	Captured by Mamluk dynasty
1241 CE	Sacking of Lahore by the Mongols
1555 CE	Comes under Mughal rule
1584 CE	Becomes a capital of the Mughal Empire at the time of Akbar
1584–1627 CE	Under the rule of Jahangir
1618–1707 CE	Under Aurangzeb

Lahore

The city of Lahore has a history of perhaps two millennia, but it came to the notice of the world only around the tenth century. From then on it became the capital of several empires including the Ghaznavis, the Delhi Sultanate and the Mughals, in whose period, between the sixteenth and eighteenth centuries it rose to become one of the world's largest cities.

Before the tenth century

***Figure 40:** Badshahi Mosque in Lahore*

there are references to Lahore but none fully confirmed. Historians and travellers such as Ptolemy and Xuanzang describe a city situated near the Chenab and Ravi Rivers which could be Lahore.

Lahore finds its first mention in the *Hudud al-Alam* (The Regions of the World) written in 982 CE. The document extols Lahore as a city with impressive temples, large markets and huge orchards.

In the eleventh century when Sultan Mahmud Ghazni captured Lahore, the city was destroyed only to be rebuilt by a Governor of the Ghaznavid Empire. Malik Ayaz, the governor of Lahore built city walls, erected a fort and repopulated the city. Under his reign, the city gained the reputation of a cultural and academic centre, renowned for its brilliant poets.

BETWEEN THE SIXTEENTH AND EIGHTEENTH CENTURIES, LAHORE ROSE TO BECOME ONE OF THE WORLD'S LARGEST CITIES

Figure 41: *Lahore fort*

When the capital of the Ghaznavid Empire, Ghazni, fell to enemy occupation in 1163, Lahore became the primary capital, leading to an influx of poets and scholars from nearby cities. But Lahore's fortune did not last long. In 1186, the last Ghaznavid ruler was overthrown and the city fell into the hands of Muhammed Ghor, the Ghurid ruler.

Following the assassination of Muhammad Ghor in 1206, Lahore changed hands once again and came into the possession of the Mamluk dynasty of the Delhi Sultanate. Lahore again flowered into a cultural centre under the reign of Qutb-ud-din-Aibak. Poets and scholars flocked to the city from as far as Turkestan, Persia and Mesopotamia. After the death of Aibak, the city came under the jurisdiction of the Governor of Multan. A period of uncertainty set in. Repeated Mongol invasions coupled with political unrest in Lahore forced rulers to shift their capital further south to a safer city such as Delhi.

The shifting of the capital to Delhi weakened the hold of the Delhi Sultanate over Lahore. The governors of the city preferred greater autonomy. But before their wish was fulfilled, Lahore was sacked by the Mongol army in 1241, forcing the governor to flee. With Lahore becoming a frontier city of the Delhi Sultanate, it suffered repeated invasions by Mongols and others. The city came under the brief rule of the Tughuq dynasty for a few years in the fourteenth century. The city was repeatedly sacked so much so that when Timur captured the city in 1398 there was nothing left to loot. The uncertain political situation in the city continued until well into the middle of the fifteenth century.

With the entry of the Moghuls into the subcontinent, Lahore attracted their attention. The city was briefly sacked by Babur in 1525. After the death of Babur when Delhi was captured by Sher Shah Suri, Babur's son Humayun had to seek refuge in Lahore in 1540 and ask for protection from its ruler Kamran Mirza, who was also his half-brother. Soon Sher Shah Suri seized Lahore too.

Humayun finally succeeded in regaining Lahore in 1555 and thereafter reached a peak in its prosperity. The Mughal presence was so strong in Lahore that more Mughal-era monuments are housed in Lahore than in Delhi.

In 1584, Lahore retained its lost glory when Akbar elevated it to the status of a capital and took measures to revive the Lahore Fort. By that time Lahore had expanded, its residential colonies spilling out of the city's walls. Akbar made his brother-in-law, Bhagwant Das, the governor of the city. Bazaars, grain markets and havelis set up during Akbar's time have survived till today. In addition, a number of mosques, tombs and shrines came up in the city during that period.

After Akbar, under his son Jahangir's (1569–1627) rule, Lahore continued to be a vibrant trade centre and a favourite of foreign traders. In 1606, Jahangir's rebel son, Khusrau Mirza, teamed up with Sikh Guru Arjan Dev to capture the city, but were repelled, ending in the martyrdom of the Sikh Guru. When the emperor died, he was buried in Lahore and a tomb erected according to his wishes.

Under Jahangir's son Shah Jahan (1592–1666) who was born in the city, Lahore saw its fort further embellished and iconic monuments such as the Naulakha Pavilion, the Shahi Hammam, the Shalimar Gardens and the Wazir Khan Mosque created. The city's suburbs expanded and the population perhaps reached its highest point during this period.

The city then passed into the hands of Aurangzeb (1618–1707), the son of Shah Jahan, who, after seizing power from his father and imprisoning him in Agra Fort, built the magnificent Alamgiri Gate. The largest of Lahore's Mughal monuments, the Badshahi Mosque, owes its existence to Aurangzeb's reign.

After Aurangzeb's death, the Mughal Empire began to wane and along with it the fortunes of Lahore declined. In the early 18th century, the Sunehri Mosque was built. The hold of Delhi over Lahore also weakened.

The tale of two cities

The cities of Lahore and Multan were constantly competing with each other during the medieval centuries. In the fourteenth century, Lahore was not well connected to trade routes going south. Lahore at this time was a ruined city offering no incentives to traders. The fortunes of Multan, on the other hand, were rising. Next to Delhi, it was considered as the most important city.

In the seventeenth century, however, the fortunes of Lahore turned for the better. It became one of the three recognised capitals of the

LAHORE'S POPULATION PERHAPS REACHED ITS HIGHEST POINT DURING THE REIGN OF SHAH JAHAN.

Figure 42: Jahangir's tomb in Shahdara Bagh, Lahore

prestigious Mughal Empire. Trade routes from Kabul and Qandahar went through Lahore, connecting it to present-day Punjab, Haryana and then to Delhi. Both Lahore and Multan prospered in this period but Multan declined in comparison to its competitor.

The Mughal state invested a considerable amount in building infrastructure, partly to improve trade routes and partly to strengthen administrative effectiveness. Under the Mughals their capitals – Lahore, Agra, Shahjahanabad (Delhi) and Fatehpur Sikri (whose life as a capital city was short-lived) prospered.

Delhi

Delhi is relatively modern compared to ancient cities such as Mathura and Pataliputra which have survived till today. The earliest archaeological layer of Delhi may be the city of Indraprastha, mentioned in the Mahabharata, whose remains in the Purana Qila stands today. Potsherds belonging to the Kushan dynasty (first to second centuries CE) have been discovered on the edges of the mound.

But the history of modern Delhi really starts from 993 CE. Since then several successive settlements or cities have been built that today are frequently referred to as the 'Seven Cities of Delhi'. They are spread over a vast landscape of 180 sq. kms containing palaces, citadels, mosques, forts, tombs and many ruined structures. There are an immense number of monuments belong to different architectural styles.

These cities of Delhi can be best grouped by the dynasties and the centuries in which they were built Qutb area Siri.

Before these cities took shape, King Anang Pal of the Tomara dynasty built Lal Kot and several temples in 1052 CE. In 1192, Muhammed Ghori defeated Prithviraj Chauhan who ruled Delhi at that time. Qutb-ud-din Aibak, the successor of Muhammed Ghori, laid the foundation of the Delhi Mamluk Sultanate. He was instrumental in building the Qutb Minar and Quwwat-al-Islam (Might of Islam) mosque, India's earliest mosque. In front of the Qutb Minar stands the Iron Pillar, a monument belonging to the Gupta period (fourth century CE) from Mathura by Qutb-ud-din.

The Mamluk Sultanate was overthrown in 1290 by Jalal-ud-din Firuz Khalji (1290–1320). Under the next Khalji ruler, Alauddin Khalji, the Delhi sultanate expanded as far south as the Narmada River in the Deccan. During this period, the fine Alai Darwaza, the walls of Siri (the second city of Delhi) and the elegant Jamaat Khana mosque were built nearer the Nizamuddin complex.

Next came the Tughlaq dynasty. Under Muhammad bin Tughluq (1325–1351), the Delhi Sultanate brought more areas under its

DELHI IS ACTUALLY MADE OF SEVEN CITIES SPREAD OVER 180 SQ KMS AND BUILT OVER FIVE CENTURIES BY DIFFERENT DYNASTIES.

Centuries	Dynasties	Cities
13th	Mamluk (1193–1290) Khilji (1290–1320)	Qutb area Siri
14th	Tughlaq (1321–1414)	Tughlaqabad Jahanpannah Firozabad
15th	Sayyid (1414–50) Lodi (1450–1526)	Mosques and tombs only
16th	Mughal (1526–40) (Babur and Humayun) Sher Shah (1540–45) Akbar (1556–1605)	Purana Qila
17th	Mughal (1605–1707) (Jehangir, Shahjahan and Aurangzeb)	Shahjahanabad
18–19th	Mughal (1707–1857) (Aurangzeb's successors)	Mosques and tombs only

control. Delhi ceased to be a capital temporarily when Tughlaq moved his capital to Daulatabad.

Under these rulers a distinctive building style developed. The third city Tughlaqabad, lying to the east of the Qutb, has an enormous palace-fortress which still stands impressively today in spite of battered walls. It was built by Ghiyasuddin Tughluq, the founder of the Tughlaq dynasty in 1321.

Mohammed Bin Tughlaq, who succeeded him, is credited with the fourth city, Jahanpannah, situated between the Qutb and Siri. This city houses the Begampur Mosque dating from Firoz Shah's time and the two adjacent structures, the Bijai Mandal and the Bara Khamba (12 pillars).

During the reign of Firoz Shah Tughlaq (1351–1388), the Delhi Sultanate started contracting. In his reign a new palace complex was built at Firoz Shah Kotla, which are sadly in ruins today. Here, surprisingly, one can find a third century BCE pillar carrying the edicts of Ashoka, brought to Delhi from Ambala by Firoz Shah. The tomb of Firoz Shah lies at Hauz Khas.

Under the Sayyid dynasty (1414–1451), the Delhi Sultanate was further reduced to Delhi and its hinterland.

It was under the Lodi dynasty (1450–1526), that the Delhi Sultanate recovered some lost areas. The Sultanate mainly ruled from Agra. The monuments of this time are mainly the tombs of the Lodi dynasty.

The Sultanate finally came to an end when Babur, the founder of the Mughal dynasty, captured Delhi early in the 16th century. Mughal dynasty ruled Delhi for more than three centuries, with just a short break during the reigns of Sher Shah Suri and Hemu from 1540 to 1556. It was Sher Shah who completed the Purana Qila, the sixth city. After Humayun's death, his tomb was built by his wife. The Persian architect who built the tomb introduced many architectural innovations that he had tried in Iran.

In Akbar's time, the capital was moved to Agra and Fatehpur Sikhri. His son Jahangir preferred Lahore over Delhi. But under Shah Jahan, Delhi regained its status as a capital. He built the city of Shahjahanabad, the present Old Delhi with its great walls and the palace-citadel, the Red Fort. The Red Fort is a majestic structure with red sandstone walls and elaborate audience halls, pavilions, private apartments, bathrooms and lawns. Nearby is the imposing Jama Masjid.

The Mughal Empire lost its pre-eminence after the death of Aurangzeb in 1707. After that it was invaded by the Marathas and the Persians. The city was again sacked by the army of Ahmad Shah Durrani in 1757. It later on came under the control of the Bharatpur State and the Sikh Empire. During this period, Raja Jai Singh built an observatory called the Jantar Mantar with enormous astronomical instruments built in masonry.

Takeaways

- Urbanization reached a peak under the Mughal Empire. Some estimates reveal that fifteen per cent of the population lived in the cities.
- There were more than a hundred cities during Akbar's reign with the population ranging from a quarter to half a million.
- Cities such as Agra, Lahore, Fatehpur Sikri, and Delhi served as Mughal capitals at one point or another.
- Cities also served as manufacturing, trading, and religious centres during this period.

Fact-check (answers at the back)

1. Agra was the capital of the Mughal Empire before Fatehpur Sikri. (Yes/No)

2. Which emperor made Fatehpur Sikri as the Mughal capital:
   a. Jahangir
   b. Aurangzeb
   c. Akbar
   d. Shah Jahan

3. According to the English traveller Ralph Fitch, the cities of Agra and Fatehpur Sikri were even greater than London. (Yes/No)

4. Shah Jahan shifted the capital of the Mughal Empire from Agra to Shahjahanabad. (Yes/No)

5. In Shah Jahan's time, Agra continued to be the second capital. (Yes/No)

Conclusion

When perusing reference material from historical sources, the question that often pops up in the reader's mind is, 'Am I reading this just for the sake of gaining more knowledge or does this have some practical use today?'

The reference material provided here on Indian cities in the ancient and medieval period should have hopefully kindled some questions in the reader's mind on what is happening to modern Indian cities today.

The Harappan cities are separated from today's cities by a long interregnum of at least 4,000 years. Yet; when we read about the excellent city planning skills of the civilizations; exquisite sanitation and drainage systems, which leaves us in awe; centralized standards and measures in construction, which have been the envy of city planners; we can easily see the relevance of our urban heritage and the possibility of learning from it.

Many may scoff at the idea of learning from civilizations who lived thousands of years back, but an understanding of the great achievements of the past would silence even virulent critics. The way Mohenjo-daro or Pataliputra, Hampi or Thanjavur stood tall among the world's best cities of their days cannot be said of our modern cities.

One would expect that 4,000 years of technological progress would have made modern cities far superior to the Harappan cities, but unfortunately, our cities are known more for their squalor, overpopulation, unplanned expansion, and other such ills rather than for their equity, aesthetics, and monuments.

It is hoped that this reference book would be of use to students, historians, city planners, and the general public.

Answers

Cities of the Harappan Civilization

1. Yes	2. Yes	3. No	4. Yes
5. No	6. a. b. c. and d.		

Cities of the Second Phase of Urbanisation

1. No	2. Yes	3. No	4. No
5. No	6. No	7. c.	8. d.

Mauryan Cities

1. Yes	2. a.	3. Yes	4. c.
5. Yes	6. b.	7. Yes	

Sangam Cities

1. No	2. No	3. No	4. No
5. Yes	6. b.	7. c.	

Early Cities of the Deccan

1. Yes	2. No	3. Yes	4. No
5. Yes	6. No	7. Yes	8. b.
9. Yes			

Capitals of the Pallavas, Chalukyas and Pandyas

1. Yes	2. No	3. Yes	4. d.
5. Yes			

Cities of the Chola Empire

1. Yes	2. Yes	3. Yes	4. Yes
5. b.			

Newer Cities of the Deccan

1. Yes	2. No	3. No	4. Yes
5. Yes	6. Yes	7. Yes	8. c.
9. d.			

Cities of the Mughal Empire

1. Yes	2. c.	3. Yes	4. Yes
5. Yes			

Reading List

Arrian, *Ancient India as described by Arrian*, excerpted from *The Indica* Archived 25 May 2012 at the Wayback Machine

Basham, A.L. [1954] 1992. *The Wonder that was IndiaI.* Rupa & Co. Delhi

Badhreenath, Dr Sathyabhama, Excavations at Adichchanallur, The Director General, Archaeological Survey Of India, New Delhi.

Caldwell, Rev. Robert. 1881. *Political and General History of the District of Tinnevelly*. Madras.

Chakrabarti, Dilip K. 2001. *The Archaeology of Ancient Indian Cities.* Delhi: Oxford University Press.

Champakalakshmi, R. 1996. *Trade, Ideology and Urbanization: South India 30 BC to AD 1300*. Delhi: Oxford University Press.

Chelliah, J.V. 1946. *Pattupattu: Ten Tamil Idylls.* Colombo: General Publishers Ltd.

Ghosh, A. (ed). 1996. *Ajanta Murals: An album of eighty-five reproductions in colour.* New Delhi: Archaeological Survey of India

Habib, Irfan. 2002. *The Indus Civilization Including Other Copper Age Cultures and History of Language Change till c. 1500 BC.* New Delhi: Tulika Books.

Haig, Lt. Col. T.W. [1907] 1919. *Historic Landmarks of the Deccan.* Allahabad: Pioneer Press.

Jouveau-Dubreuil, G. 1920. *Ancient History of the Deccan.* Pondicherry.

Karashima, Noboru. 2014. *A Concise History of South India: Issues and Interpretations.* New Delhi: Oxford University Press.

Lal, B.B. [1954] 1955. *Excavation at Hastinapura and Other Explorations in the Upper Ganga and Sutlej Basins, 1950–52.* Ancient India 10,11: 5–151.

Mahalingam, T.V. 1969. *Kanchipuram in Early South Indian History.* Madras: Asia Publishing House.

Pigott, Stuart. 1945. *Some Ancient Cities of India.* London: Oxford University Press.

Pliny the Elder. 1855. *The Natural History*, Translated By John Bostock, and H. T. Riley, Vol. II. London: H.G. Bohn.

Possehl, Gregory L. 2003. *The Indus Civilisation: A Contemporary Perspective.* New Delhi: Vikas Publishing House.

Ray, Nihar-Ranjan. 1945. *Maurya and Sunga Art.* University of Calcutta.

Raychaudhuri, Tapan and Habib, Irfan (ed.), *The Cambridge Economic History of India, Volume I: C. 1200-C. 1750,* 1982: Cambridge University Press.

Rowland, Benjamin. [1953] 1984. *The Art and Architecture of India: Buddhist, Hindu, Jain.* New York: Penguin.

Sastri, K. A. Nilakanta. [1955] 1975. *A History of South India from Prehistoric Times to the Fall of Vijaynagar.* 4th edn. Madras. Oxford University Press.

Sharma, R.S. [2005] 2016. *India's Ancient Past.* New Delhi: OUP.

Singh, Upinder. 2009. *A History of Ancient and Early Medieval India.* Delhi: Pearson.

2004a.'Cults and Shrines in Early Historical Mathura (*c.* 200 BC–AD 200).' *World Archaeology* 36(3): 378–98.

Sivanantham, Dr R (ed.). Seran, M. (ed.), *Keeladi: An Urban Settlement of Sangam Age on the banks of river Vaigai*, Chennai: Department of Archaeology, Government of Tamil Nadu

Thakur, Vijay Kumar. 1981. *Urbanization in Ancient India*. New Delhi Abhinav Publications.

Thapar, Romila. [1963] 1987. *Aśoka and the Decline of the Mauryas*. 7th rep. Delhi: Oxford University Press.

Vasudeva S. Agrawala (1965). *Masterpieces of Mathura Sculpture*. Prithivi Prakashan, Varanasi.

Wheeler, Mortimer. 1962. *Charsada: A Metropolis of The North-West Frontier*. OUP.

Zvelebil, Kamil V. 1974. Tamil Literature In Jan Honda (ed.), A History of Indian Literature. Vol. X. Fasc. 1. Wiesbaden: Otto Harrassowitz.

Index

Image Copyright Information

Figures from Shutterstock.com:
1, 7, 9, 16, 19, 21, 22, 23, 24, 25, 26, 27, 28, 29, 30, 31, 32, 33, 34, 35, 36, 37, 38, 39, 40, 41, 42

Figures from Wikipedia.org:
4 (Fair Use),
5 (CC BY-SA 3.0),
3 (CC BY-SA 3.0/Saqib Qayyum),
10 (CC BY 3.0/Biswarup Ganguly),
11 (Public Domain),
12 (Public Domain),
13 (CC BY 3.0/ Biswarup Ganguly),
14 (Public Domain),

Figures from Wikimedia Commons:
2 (CC BY-SA 3.0/Usman),
6 (GODL),
8 (CC BY-SA 4.0/Orissa8),
15 (CC BY-SA 4.0/SarahWelch),
17 (Public Domain),
18 (CCA-SA 4.0/Paramatamil),
20 (CCA-SA 4.0/Paramatamil)

Acknowledgements

This book is a tribute to all those archaeologists, historians and the stray travellers who helped locate and unearth priceless information about our ancient and medieval cities, often buried under many layers of occupation and repeated vandalisation.

Places such as Mohenjo-daro, Harappa and Kanchipuram have evoked in me the yearning to learn about our ancient cities with their rich heritage from my school days. Glimpses of these cities from school text books survived in my memory until I had a chance to visit a few of them in later years. Every visit to archaeological sites of dead cities and to the monuments and markets of age-old living cities evoked in me a sharp desire to learn more about their antecedents, the people who inhabited them in faraway times, their cultures, language, attire and other preoccupations. Over a period of time, I started collecting material related to these cities.

Finally, the opportunity arrived to write a short and modest publication on these splendorous cities. This publication is by no means an exhaustive, original account of the cities included here. The material used here has been drawn from some classical works related to our ancient and medieval cities. These documents open up whole new vistas for further exploration into the history of our ancient cities.

I express my immense gratitude to Anirban Sarkar of Hachette India whose endearing engagement and inexhaustible patience has contributed to the final shape of this book. I also thank his colleagues Anupama Manral, Yukta Vats and the rest of the team for their invaluable contribution to this publication.

Finally, I cannot end this note without thanking my wife, Vidya Raghavan, and son, Srinath Raghavan, whose critical feedback and profuse advice kept up my spirits.

Raghavan Srinivasan
New Delhi, August 2023